21 Stories
Of
AULD ABERDEEN

by
John A. Henderson

with illustrations by
John Mackay

Terror as the Dee Ferry capsizes

(See page 70)

introduction

Helpless citizens watch as a ship is dashed to pieces by giant seas and 42 sailors drown ... drunken soldiers open fire on the streets killing and maiming innocent folk ... kirk ministers say an earthquake which hits the city is caused by the sinful lives led by inhabitants such as fishing for salmon on a Sunday ... thirty two passengers are lost as the ferry crossing the Dee sinks ... university students riot at the installation of their new rector ... an expedition sails from the town in search of lost Arctic explorers.

These are just some of the headline making stories from Aberdeen's past which are featured in this facsimile reprint of "Twenty One Aberdeen Events of the Nineteenth Century" by John A. Henderson ("Aberdeen Daily Journal". 1912).

The author was a well known writer on antiquarian and historical subjects. He compiled an index to the "Journal" for the first one hundred years of its existence between 1747 and 1847 and his other published works included "Annals of Lower Deeside", "Aberdeenshire Epitaphs and Inscriptions" and "History of the Society of Advocates in Aberdeen".

In a foreword to the original edition Mr Henderson wrote; "The occurrence of various incidents as narrated in the following chapters created such a widespread interest that no excuse need be offered for the publication of this volume.

"Its pages furnish, in concise form, the dates and particulars which the Publishers are asked for by correspondents almost daily".

For this issue John Mackay has produced a set of new drawings to illustrate the stories.

Others featured tell of:—

★ The wrecking of the SS Duke of Sutherland at the mouth of Aberdeen Harbour on April 1, 1853. Sixteen are lost.

★ Further drama when the SS Brilliant, a regular trading steamer which plied between Leith and Aberdeen for 18 years, sinks at the same spot in a hurricane.

★ The widows and orphans of the railway: three arches of a new viaduct give way and their men are buried in the rubble.

★ Disaster at the theatre ... off-stage. It burns down. Seven are dead; 30 injured.

★ Terrific gales sweep Scotland in November and December of 1876 with the loss of 63 vessels and 294 lives. How does Aberdeen cope?

★ Fire destroys the New Market Building. The blaze "is materially increased through the melting of the gas pipes ... the fire quickly runs along each gallery, devouring toys, clothing, hardware, books and other commodities on sale in the various stalls".

★ Citizens give a stylish response when Queen Victoria stops off for a visit en route to the Royal Family's new holiday home at Balmoral.

★ How the Great North of Scotland Railway provided Aberdeen and surrounding counties with a most efficient rail service.

★ The day the fire brigade fell down on the job.

COVER ILLUSTRATION: An old view of Aberdeen looking from the South.

Published by Lang Syne Publishers Ltd
45 Finnieston St., Glasgow
Tel: 041-204 3104
Printed by Dave Barr Print
45 Finnieston Street, Glasgow
Tel: 041-221 2598

Reprinted 1992

ANGRY SOLDIERS GUN DOWN INNOCENT CITIZENS

June 4, 1802

THE harmony and good feeling usually existing between the military stationed from time to time at Aberdeen and the residenters received a rude check on the occasion of the king's birthday, on Friday, June 4, 1802.

As customary on that day, the civic authorities invited the officers of the Highland regiment at the barracks (the Ross and Cromarty Rangers) to the Town Hall to drink his Majesty's health. The commander and several other officers attended; but, unfortunately, they indulged too freely in wine, and soon became intoxicated. On their return to the barracks their condition was noticed by some idle lads who had congregated on the Castlegate, and were amusing themselves by "throwing squibs, dirt, and garbage at each other, but in other respects not inclined to mischief nor much disposed to riot." The boys stupidly threw some of the garbage at the officers, who got intensely irritated at the supposed indignity. Instead of walking on, endeavouring to conciliate the boys, or lodging a complaint with the authorities, the officers at once took the law into their own hands, and without the sanction or the presence of a civil magistrate, as legally required, called out the regiment from the barracks, with a view to actively resenting the fancied insults to which they had been subjected. The consequence was that in a very short time " a tumult and disorder ensued, and the populace and the military

B

became exasperated at each other." The soldiers, considering themselves for the moment free from discipline, and unrestrained by their officers, repeatedly fired with ball cartridge upon the people in the Castlegate, four of whom were killed and many wounded. The magistrates, now greatly alarmed, exerted their authority, and commanded the military to retire to their barracks, the soldiers being thus prevented from committing further mischief.

The atrocious act of a military force firing indiscriminately upon an unarmed populace, and that without the slightest warning to disperse, raised much feeling in the public mind. The ire of the people became thoroughly roused, and they vowed to have vengeance on the regiment, to avert the perpetration of which the soldiers were kept closely within barracks and ultimately marched out of the city at midnight, each man being on his stocking soles to deaden the sound.

Meantime, several of the officers and soldiers prominently implicated in the riot were apprehended and lodged in prison, on a warrant issued by the magistrates, on a charge of wilful murder. Precognitions of witnesses on all the phases of the subject were then taken and transmitted to the Crown authorities at Edinburgh ; but the Lord Advocate, on full consideration, refused to order a criminal prosecution, and he consented to the liberation of those in custody on their finding security to stand trial, when called upon, at any time within six months.

These circumstances strongly agitated the public mind and excited the discontent of the people, who argued, with apparent good reason, that, as the lives of so many citizens had been sacrificed by the culpable conduct of the military, a public trial was indispensably necessary for the sake of public justice, whatever might be its final issue. Many of the principal citizens, therefore, arranged to prosecute the case in the names of the parents of those who had been killed, and to raise such sums of money by voluntary subscription as might be deemed adequate to defray the expenses. The machinery of the law being thus set in motion, the trial of three of the officers and two sergeants, who were considered the most blameworthy, commenced in the High Court of Justiciary at Edinburgh on July 6, 1803, and continued for several days thereafter. The result was that the jury found two of the officers not guilty, and the libel, so far as it concerned the two sergeants, not proven. The other officer, who had absconded, was outlawed for non-appearance.

As pointed out by Kennedy in his " Annals of Aberdeen," this unexpected result was greatly displeasing to the citizens, nor could it fail to mortify them exceedingly. " What added still more to their vexation, they found themselves involved in an enormous expense to lawyers, agents, and their retainers at Edinburgh, to which the voluntary subscriptions were by no means adequate. This expense exceeded £900 sterling, exclusive of the personal charges of many of the witnesses . . ."

The following is the " Aberdeen Journal's " account of the proceedings :—

On Friday last the anniversary of his Majesty's Birthday was observed in this city with the usual marks of joy. At twelve, three volleys were fired by the Ross and Cromarty Rangers in the Barrack-yard ; and the young men of the different Incorporations made a procession through the town with their colours and the insignia of their different trades, and made a very showy appearance. At six o'clock the magistrates and principal inhabitants assembled in the Town Hall, where the usual healths and other appropriate toasts were drank, followed by repeated volleys of musketry by a detachment of the military drawn up on the Plainstones. Thus far the day was spent with that festivity which has long distinguished the inhabitants of this loyal city. But it now becomes our painful duty to relate the melancholy events of the evening, which led to consequences that we can never sufficiently deplore. An unfortunate affray took place between the boys in the street and some of the officers and privates of the Ross and Cromarty Rangers, then on guard in Castle Street, who, being joined by the rest of the corps from the barracks, ran upon the people in the street with their arms in their hands, and began firing upon them with ball, indiscriminately and in every direction, and some were even seen taking deliberate aim at individuals. Many of the bullets went through windows and doors in the west end of Castle Street and in the head of the Shiprow and Narrow Wynd, and others were found at a greater distance through the town. As far as we can learn, the following were the fatal consequences that ensued—One man, a native of this place, and a private in the Rifle corps recruiting here, who was standing at the corner of the Planestones, was shot through the head, and instantly died on the spot. Thomas Milne, a mason; John Moir, a young boy, and only son of a widow; and William Gibb, apprentice to a barber, were all mortally wounded, and died next day; and ten more persons, as near as we can learn, were variously wounded. Upon being informed of the unhappy affair, the Provost and Magistrates, with becoming spirit, instantly interfered, and the whole corps were ordered into the barracks. A sufficient guard of armed citizens was immediately mounted, to prevent all communication with the regiment, which, in the irritated state of the public mind, might have led to further fatal consequences. An investigation of this lamentable affair was instantly set on foot by the magistrates, and is now going on . . .

On Saturday at twelve o'clock an express was sent off to Edinburgh to the Commander in Chief. The person, who carried it with an alacrity which did him much credit, returned again by three o'clock on Monday morning with the necessary orders; and yesterday morning about one o'clock the regiment marched out of town in dead silence and without beat of drum by the way of the Broadhill and Old-town Links, on their route northwards. . . .

Soldiers open fire on citizens

The 'Oscar' goes down in a violent storm

FORTY TWO DIE AS FREAK STORM WRECKS THE 'OSCAR'

April 1, 1813

N Thursday, April 1, 1813, after a tract of exceptionally fine weather, there arose a sudden and violent storm, which, although brief in its duration, caused one of the most melancholy and unexpected shipwrecks that have ever occurred in connection with the port of Aberdeen. In the morning the wind, which had been westerly during the night, veered round to the south-east, with snow, but shifted soon after to the north-eastward. At this time five of the whale-fishing ships belonging to Aberdeen—the Hercules, Latona, Middleton, St. Andrew, and Oscar, which had sailed early in the morning—were riding at anchor in the bay; and the weather being still unsettled, and having the appearance of an impending storm, the two last mentioned, about five o'clock, weighed anchor and stood out to sea. A boat from the Oscar having gone ashore for some of her belated crew, the vessel put about, stood into the bay, and succeeded in getting the last of her hands aboard. By this time the Oscar was far in shore; and a fatal calm, with a heavy rolling sea and strong flood tide coming in, rendered it impracticable to clear the Girdleness. The vessel continuing to fall to the leeward, had to be brought up in the face of the rocky shore, within the Ness, soon after which the increasing violence of the gale, with its thick snowfall, rendered her position extremely precarious, and filled the minds of the people on shore with painful apprehension. Shortly after eleven a.m. the Oscar was driven ashore in the Greyhope, immediately behind the breakwater, at the south side of the harbour. A number of the townspeople at once set out for the wreck, and getting across by the ferry, were soon on the spot, prepared to render such assistance as might be possible in the circumstances. The heart-rending scene which presented itself, however, made it too apparent that all human efforts to preserve the ship and the lives of the unfortunate crew would prove unavailing. The vessel lay among large submerged rocks, and consequent upon the tremendous seas which were steadily breaking over her, was rapidly breaking up.

An attempt made by the crew to form a sort of bridge to the nearest high rocks by cutting away the mainmast proved abortive, through its falling alongside instead of towards the shore as anticipated. Many of the brave fellows who had clung to the rigging were now, through the falling of the fore and mizzen masts, plunged into the sea, where they quickly perished. Others, having nothing stable to hold by, were swept off the wreck, and they sank in sight of those on shore, who were unable to render the least assistance, even although the intervening distance was quite trifling. A few who had almost struggled ashore were swept back by the heavy surf, or borne down by the wreckage from the ship.

The forecastle still remaining above water, five men were observed (among them the master, Captain John Innes, making urgent signals for assistance) clinging to it; but the whole vessel having speedily gone to pieces they shared the sad fate of their companions. John Jamson, first mate, and James Venus, seaman, belonging to Shields, were the only survivors of a crew of forty-four. The rescue of Jamson was effected under striking circumstances. His uncle, Captain Richard Jamson (great-grandfather of Rev. James Smith, St. George's-in-the-West, Aberdeen), was among the crowd attracted to the spot, and observing an object floating in the boiling surf, he reached out his staff and had it pulled ashore. It turned out to be his own nephew, and the vigorous efforts made to bring him round were happily successful.

The Oscar, with her superior equipment, was valued at £10,000, but this was considered infinitesimal in proportion to the loss of the forty-two hardy seamen, who only a few hours before had left their happy homes and friends with the brightest prospects for a successful voyage. The sympathies of the populace went forth in no unstinted fashion to the bereaved, and sums were raised in various ways. The domestic servants of the city contributed handsomely, and a special performance in the theatre yielded some £80.

Mr. William Robbie, in the account of the wreck he gives in his book on " Aberdeen," says—" The gale soon grew into a hurricane, and the snow-drift became so thick and blinding that the strongest men could with difficulty bear up against the force of the tempest. People who had a distinct recollection of the day have said that a kind of awe seemed to fall on many of the inhabitants at the preternatural suddenness and violence of the storm, accompanied with a strange dread that some dire calamity was impending."

A local bard contributed the following ode on the sad disaster to the " Aberdeen Journal " of April 7, 1813 :—

> What sounds are these that strike my listening ear
>   In the dread pauses of the furious blast
> Which, with the speed of lightning, does career
> Across the darkened sky ? Methinks I hear
>   The mournful cry
>   Of death and hopeless misery.
>
> Yes, April ! though thou'rt wont, like the world's guile,
> To gild with sunny smile
>   The cloud which nurses in its breast
> The rattling hail or chilly shower,
> To blast the opening bud and flower ;
> Yet now thou comest, borne on December's car,
>   Urged on thy way by the rude blustering storm ;
> And, with the fury of the winter's war,
> Sweepest the raging sea—
> The messenger of God, charged with His dread decree.
>
> The gallant ship, prepared to brave
> The northern ocean's mighty wave ;
> Her jovial crew, with thoughtless glee,
> Draining the parting cup right merrily,
>   Last setting sun beheld :
> Yet never more, on ship or men,
> The setting sun shall look again.

In sight of home, how hard to die !
In sight of home, to raise the cry
Of wild despair, and friends so nigh !

April ! full many a widow's moan and orphan's tear,
For the lost spouse and father dear ;
    Full many a mother's breaking heart
Shall rue thy morning's awful rage,
And mark, with anguish keen, thy name in memory's page.

Mr. William Cadenhead also composed a long poem upon the disaster.

The bodies of the crew, as recovered, were reverently interred in various churchyards, including those of Nigg, St. Nicholas, and Newburgh. A tombstone in the last mentioned is inscribed :—

Sacred to the memory of Captain John Innes, aged 42 years, who was wrecked in the ship Oscar, near Aberdeen, the 1st April, 1813. This stone is erected by his disconsolate widow, Ann Mitchell, as a grateful tribute of her regard and affection for his departed worth. Their son, Thomas, who died in infancy, is also interred here.

Though Boreas' blasts and Neptune's waves
    Have toss'd me to and fro,
In spite of both, by God's decree,
    I harbour here below.
Here at an anchor I do lie,
    With many of our fleet,
Untill again we most set sail,
    Our Admiral Christ to meet.

Also his spouse, Ann Mitchell, who died the 16th November, 1828, aged 68 years.

It may be of interest to state that Captain and Mrs. Innes executed a mutual deed of settlement on March 15, 1811, one of the conditions of which bore that, on the death of the longest liver of the two, each of the children of George and Alexander Innes (brothers of Captain Innes), both shipmasters in Aberdeen, should have an annuity of £40.

A storm very similar to that just described, adds Mr. Robbie, occurred on January 26, 1815, and was likewise attended with much loss of life. The brig, Caledonia, foundered at the mouth of the harbour, and her crew of seven persons were drowned. In seeking safety from the same tempest, the schooner, Providence, was wrecked, and her crew perished; and the trading smack, Thames, was driven among the rocks almost at the same spot where the Oscar had been lost, her crew and passengers, nine persons in all, sharing the same fate.

Seven drown as the Caledonia founders
at the mouth of the harbour

GOD PUNISHES SINNERS
WITH AN EARTHQUAKE!

August 13, 1816

THE following particulars of an earthquake which occurred in the city and neighbourhood are recorded by Kennedy in his "Annals of Aberdeen" :—

On Tuesday, the 13th of August, 1816, a shock of an earthquake was distinctly felt in the various quarters of this town and in the neighbourhood. This awful visitation took place at four minutes before eleven o'clock in the evening, and continued nearly six seconds. The undulation seemed to come from S.S.E., and was simultaneously felt to the distance of some miles in the direction of N.N.W. The houses in many parts of the town were shaken to their foundations; the heaviest articles of furniture in them were moved; and a rumbling noise was heard, as if some heavy body was rolling along their roofs. In many of them the bells were set a-ringing, and the agitation of the wires continued visible for some time after the cessation of the shock. In about three-quarters of an hour afterwards another, but slighter shock, was distinctly felt. The air during the remainder of the night was mild and serene, with clear moonlight; and the only extraordinary appearance after the shocks was that of a thin, whitish vapour settling on the surrounding hills. Fortunately, although it created a considerable degree of alarm among the inhabitants, no damage was occasioned to any of the buildings in the town. This is the only instance of any shock of an earthquake having been felt in this quarter since the 8th of September, (*sic*) 1608, when an incident of the same nature occurred, and seemed to have been attended with similar effects.

The "Aberdeen Journal," in commenting upon the incident, adds that the agitation had been described "by one who was in Lisbon at that period as exactly resembling the commencement of the earthquake in that city on the 6th of June, 1807." It is further added that a "second, but more partial shock, was felt at half-past eleven, since which time (blessed be God) we have had no return of this awful and, in our happy country, unusual visitation of His Providence."

At Inverness, where the undulations seem to have been felt severely, great excitement prevailed. Almost every inhabitant flew to the streets, "women and children screaming, and a very considerable proportion of them naked." Some ran to the adjoining fields, where they remained for the remainder of the night.

The following record of the earthquake which occurred in Aberdeen on 8th November, 1608, and referred to by Kennedy in the foregoing account, is preserved in the Session Register of Aberdeen (vol. ii., 1602 to 1609), and is here given as showing the construction which people then put upon such a visitation, and the method the church adopted to turn it to practical account :—

Wednesday, the Nynt of November, 1608.
The Bischop, Moderator.

The quhilk day, The ministers and sessioun, convening in the Session-hous, considdering the fearfull Erthquak that wis yister-nicht, the aucht of this instant, throughout this haill Citie, about nyne hours at evin, to be a a document that God is angrie aganes the Land, and aganes this Citie in particular, for the manifauld sinnis of the people : Theirfor appoyntis and ordanis a solemne Fast and Humiliation of all the Inhabitantis of this Brught, to be the morne, quhilk is Thuirsday ; and the Covenant to be renewit be the haill people, both ministers, magistrattis, and comunitie, with God, be haulding up of thair handis all publictlie befoir God in his sanctuarie, and promesing be his grace to forbear in tyme cumming from thair sinnis that hes procuret Goddis wraith and anger aganes thame.

Decimo-tertio Novembris, 1608.

The quhilk day efter incalling of God, Peter, bischop off Aberdene, moderatour, exponit and declarit to the magistrattis and Sessioun that amangis the manyfauld and innumerable sinnis of this Citie that procuris Goddis wraith, the sin of bracking and prophaning of the Lordis Saboth, be publict and opin salmond fisching thairon, cheiflie procuris the same, quhilk, howbeit, it hes bene from tyme to tyme condampnit and forbidden be the licht of Goddis word : yet the possessours of the watteris preferring, as apperis, thair greid and avarice to the glorie and wirschip of God, hawe continewit and persistit hitherto in working and fisching of thair watteris on the Saboth-day, to the heich dishonour of God, the manifest contempt of his law, and sclander of the Gospell : and becaus the visitatioun of the Citie drawis nier, God being threatning the same, pairtlie be the Plague of Pestilence alredie enterit in the toune of Torrie, on the vther syd of the watter, and paritlie be a fearfull Erthquak, quhilk wis universallie throughout this Citie, and in many pairtis to landwart, on Tuysday last, the aucht of this instant . . . to the great terrour of the people that felt and persaved the samen. It becummis the people of all rankis to turne to God, and to leave thair sinnis, speciallie these publict and rebellious sinnes quhilk postis on Goddis judge-mentis aganes us ; and for this effect, be advyse of the magistrattis, he had causit warne, to this day, the possessouris of the Townis watteris to vnder-stand and knaw of thame gif they will willinglie promeas to forbear,in tyme cumming all working or laboring of thair salmound fischings on the Saboth-day ; and they being callet comperit the possessouris efter-folowing, quha being inquired be the moderatour gif they would sanctifie the Lord's Saboth, disist be thameselffs, and theair servandis, from working and fisching of thair salmound fischings thairon in tyme cumming, that God may be honored, and his judgementis, threatened aganis ws for that sin in speciall, amangs many vther sinnis, may be averted, anserit as efter folowis, to wit. The maist pairt comperand, promeist absolutelie to forbear, both be thamselffs and thair servandis, in tyme cumming ; vtheris promeist to forbear vpon the conditioun subscryvent ; and sum plainlie refuissit anyway to forbear ; and sum wer not yet throughlie resolved.

The names of those that hawe promeist absolutelie, for thamselffs and thair servandis, to desist :—

Alex. Cullen, Provost.
Alex. Rutherfurd.
John Collison.
Mr. Alex. Cullen.
William Lowsoun.
Alex. Jaffray.
Thomas Forbes, younger.
Alex. Kempt.
Mr. Gilbert Gray.
Mr. Robert Mar.

Mr. William Reid.
Patrick Gray.
Patrick Donaldson.
Martin Howison.
David Cargill.
William Gray.
George Anderson.
Mr. Andro Clerk.
Alex. Rolland.
Alex. Anderson.

Terror as an earthquake grips the city

FIRST PADDLE STEAMER BUILT IN ABERDEEN

April 12, 1827

SHIP-BUILDING has been prosecuted at Aberdeen to a greater or less extent for a lengthened period. On February 26, 1606, Alexander Davidson, timber merchant, St. Andrews, having purchased from the woods of Drum as much timber as would build " ane bark." craved authority from the Town Council of Aberdeen to build the ship in the kirkyard of the Trinity Friars. The application being deemed " verie reasonable," the necessary authority was granted. The Aberdeen-built clippers for a time enjoyed a world-wide reputation, alike for proportion, stability, and speed, but the superior and more reliable sailing powers attained through the introduction of steam have rendered steamers the more popular.

It was not till 1826-27 that an effort was made to build a paddle steamer at the port. The forward movement was undertaken by Messrs. John Duffus & Co., Footdee, and as may be supposed, their action attracted the keenest possible interest. The size of the vessel, when compared with such modern liners as the Olympic and Mauretania, pales into insignificance; but we give the description in the words of one who witnessed the launch, which took place on April 12, 1827 :—

On Thursday last we had the gratification of being present at the launch of the first steam vessel which has been built at this port. If we may judge by the admiration which this magnificent ship has excited among naval and scientific persons, as well as those acquainted with steam navigation, we may safely pronounce her the finest of her class— not only for a frame of timber which cannot be surpassed, but which has been put together in a manner that would do credit to any of the King's dock-yards. The length is that of a 36-gun frigate; she has a spar deck and poop, with two splendid cabins, separate from the sleeping apartments, which are ranged along the sides of the ship, and all entering from the main deck.   These berths have removing stanchions, which, if necessary, would enable her to carry 15 guns on a side.   She will be propelled by two engines of seventy-five horse power each, and is calculated to carry, besides her machinery, fuel, etc., three hundred tons.

Notwithstanding the unfavourable state of the weather from incessant rain, a vast concourse of spectators had assembled at an early hour, and seemed delighted with some beautiful airs played by the band of the Aberdeenshire Militia.   At a quarter past one o'clock the Queen of Scotland majestically glided into·her future element, amidst the cheers of the multitude, the band playing "God Save the King."   This superb vessel has been built by Messrs. J. Duffus & Co., and her engines constructed at their extensive establishment here; and if the Queen of Scotland is to be considered a fair specimen of their work, it will bear a comparison with that of any of her class in the kingdom.   The launch was conducted by Mr. Ronald, the master-builder, in a style which did him great credit; and we were much pleased to see the accommodation afforded by the proprietors of the neighbouring dock-yards, whose servants appeared to vie with each other in rendering every assistance in their power on this novel occasion.   .   .   .

It was not till Saturday, August 25, that the trial trip was made.   Even then the work was far from completion, it being necessary to take 120 mechanics on board.   As it blew fresh, it was found impossible to land them till the following afternoon.   They rendered good service in extinguishing a fire which broke out about midnight.   Little damage was done, and the vessel was shortly afterwards placed on the regular run between Aberdeen and London.

100 TOBACCO BOYS JOIN GREAT 'REFORM' MARCH

May 23, 1831

CITIZENS of Aberdeen have always shown a keen interest in political affairs, and the interest appears to have increased greatly during the decade preceding the passing of the Reform Bill of 1832.

The city was formerly grouped with the burghs of Montrose, Brechin, Arbroath, and Bervie in having the privilege to return one representative to the British Parliament.

An election took place on Monday, May 23, 1831, when Mr. Horatio Ross, of Rossie, a strenuous advocate for Parliamentary reform, was returned without opposition. The opportunity was embraced by the citizens of Aberdeen, not only for showing their favour and goodwill to Mr. Ross, but also their sympathy with and desire for reform. It was accordingly arranged by the Reform Committee of the Burgesses, and by that of the Trades and working classes, that they should assemble for the purpose of meeting and escorting Mr. Ross to town. The following is extracted from the graphic account of the proceedings furnished by the '' Aberdeen Journal of May 25 following :—

The most extensive and magnificent preparations were made; and we have now the satisfaction of adding that the whole were carried into effect with a degree of splendour, of order, and of regularity, of which the annals of our good city furnish no previous example.

As early as six o'clock in the morning the note of preparation sounded in all directions; banners, with inscriptions suitable to the occasion, were displayed in several parts of the town, along Union Street, and on the road leading to the Bridge of Dee; and various parties of the working classes were seen hurrying in their gayest attire to the places where they had appointed to assemble. Before eight o'clock the Incorporated Trades and working classes had nearly all met, each trade accompanied by a separate band of music, and bearing the usual emblems of their craft, together with many spirited inscriptions denoting their loyalty and warm wishes for the success of the reform cause.

About half-past eight the whole marched out, preceded by a trumpeter on horseback, followed by Mr. Cooke, also on a beautiful horse, and drew up in Union Street. It would be invidious to descant upon the superiority of one trade over another; but we cannot help remarking on the elegant appearance of the carpet weavers, who, in addition to most appropriate flags, were almost uniform in dress, and wore squares of carpeting as aprons, of the most beautiful designs and workmanship. Their brethren, the cotton weavers, also mustered strongly, wearing uniformly white and beautifully mounted aprons. Then there were the tanners and curriers, a numerous body, dressed uniformly in tan-coloured trousers, shirts, and aprons, and blue bonnets; their appearance was exceedingly striking. Then came the gardeners—most beautiful, because most natural, of all—having in their party upwards of a dozen beautifully decorated crowns composed of flowers, and other emblems. In addition to all the young men belonging to the Incorporated Trades, there were parties of every occupation which we could mention, not omitting the tobacco boys, poor little fellows, who mustered to the number of 100, all neat and clean, wearing white aprons, and headed by an American Black, the usual sign of the trade. In short, the walking part of the procession was beyond description—tasteful and elegant, and evinced that the managers of it had spared no pains to show every mark of esteem for the cause and its supporter, Mr. Ross.

By half-past eight, the gentlemen of the Reform Committee had assembled at the Royal Hotel door . . . and, having taken their seats in the carriages, each of which was drawn by four horses, and having the postilions, horses, etc., decorated with flowers, and the usual

c

election insignia of party-coloured ribbons, the Procession started for the Bridge of Dee in the following order, the bands playing, and the banners reflecting the sun's rays in the most dazzling manner. First, the committee of the working classes; then the working classes, all in their best clothes, or wearing the habiliments of their respective professions; then the Incorporated Trades in appropriate costumes; and lastly, in carriages decorated as above, the gentlemen of the Reform Committee. These carriages amounted to about twenty. . . .

The cavalcade having reached the Bridge of Dee, its march thither enlivened by the music of the various bands, the cheers of the populace, and the firing of artillery placed on the eminences in the vicinity of the bridge, the working classes made a halt, and allowed the trades to pass on to the other side of the river, where they remained drawn up in lines on each side of the road, to allow the carriages that closed the procession to pass on between them, and join Mr. Ross on his arrival. At this time the procession itself, and the dense multitude of spectators that had turned out to witness it, extended upwards of two miles in length, and might have been fairly estimated at above 30,000 persons of both sexes, of all ranks, young and old. On Mr. Ross's arrival, about ten o'clock, the air was rent with the loudest cheers, and the honourable gentleman and his attendants seemed struck with astonishment and overwhelmed with gratitude at the welcome he received.

It need only be stated further that the ovation and cordial reception continued all the way to Castle Street, where, in the Town Hall, Mr Ross was unanimously and most heartily returned as M.P.

Citizens march for local democracy

VICTORIA'S CORONATION — ABERDEEN REJOICES

June 28, 1838

EADERS of history know with what goodwill and heartiness the people of past generations were wont to enjoy themselves, and how readily they responded to calls for public rejoicing. The following graphic account of the festivities held in Aberdeen on the occasion f the Coronation of Queen Victoria, on June 28, 1838, is given in the " Aberdeen Journal " of July 4 following.

The confident anticipations which we entertained of the eclat with which her Majesty's Coronation would be celebrated in " brave Aberdeen " have been completely realized. Never on any occasion of public rejoicing have we beheld more perfect success of previous arrangements, or evidence of a better spirit pervading all classes of the community, than were displayed here on Thursday last. The whole of the proceedings were creditable in the highest degree to the good taste and judgment of those who directed them, while the loyalty, good feeling, and orderly behaviour of the thousands who thronged the streets of this city are beyond all praise. Everyone seemed pleased with himself and with all about him, and the happiness of the whole was enhanced by the interchange of goodwill and kindly offices between individuals of all ranks and denominations. The weather was remarkably propitious; not a cloud curtained the sky, while a refreshing breeze, in the early part of the day, mitigated the oppressiveness of the summer sun.

At day dawn, the bells of the city were clamorous with notes of joy. The Union Jack, associated with so many reminiscences of national

glory, was unfurled on the battlements of the Town House; the vessels
in the Harbour were decorated with a profusion of flags; while banners
of every hue and device waved in various quarters of the city. The
Union Jack which was hoisted on the top of Messrs. Hadden's new
and stupendous chimney, at a height of nearly 200 feet from the ground,
had a remarkably fine effect. Two fine *jets d'eau*—the one in Castle
Street, in the form of an imperial crown, with the letters "V.R."
underneath; the other in the Green, framed on some mysterious
principle of hydraulic science—performed their respective parts to the
admiration of all beholders.

By ten o'clock the city was all a-gog. Crowds of well-dressed
citizens, young and old, gentle and simple, bustled along the streets
to the various points of attraction. Business was generally suspended
all the shops being closed. The various "crafts" which were to take
part in the grand procession, now began to move from the places of
their assembling to the general rendezvous at the Inches. The pro
cession having been formed agreeably to programme, began to march
to the sound of martial music along the prescribed route. The whole
had a very impressing effect. The different trades seemed to vie with
each other in the splendour of their decorations. We are at a loss to
say to which the palm of superiority ought to be assigned, where each
had done its best. The Hammermen, the Tailors, the Bakers, the
Fleshers, the Carpet Weavers, the Gardeners, etc., were all splendidly
adorned with the appropriate emblems of their respective Trades. There
were "Kings" in triumphal cars, and "Princes" on foot, with
gorgeous trains, supported by numerous "pages"; "warriors," mailed
to the teeth; and reverend "clerks," wigged and gowned, with
"spectacles on nose," all doing their honours in most creditable style
The Gardeners were particularly fine, their decorations being redolent of
the choicest gifts of Flora, diffusing fragrance wherever they approached
The Carpet Weavers seemed determined to outdo all their former doing
on similar occasions. They mustered to the number of 260, all resplen

dent in the most beautiful specimens of their handiwork. A triumphal car, decorated with splendid emblazonments of the city arms and other devices—all from the loom—was drawn slowly along by remarkably fine horses, mounted by riders in foreign costume, whose bearing attracted particular notice. Within the car was a band of musicians, who sent forth sweet melody, "Unseen, but not remote." "His Majesty" must have felt some inconvenience from the trappings of "Royalty," robed as he was in carpeting from top to toe. The whole body, on the conclusion of the procession, were regaled in the great square of Messrs. Hadden's works in the Green, when the healths of her Majesty, and the highly-respectable employers of the operatives, were drank with the utmost enthusiasm. The Firemen of the North of Scotland Assurance Company, with one of their Engines, drawn by six beautiful caparisoned horses, formed part of the procession. In passing the Town House, the procession paused to pay a mark of respect to our worthy Provost (Mr. James Milne) by greeting him with three hearty cheers, which he acknowledged with his usual affability and kindness. The pageant passed along the principal streets in the city and neighbourhood, not omitting a visit to the "Auld Town," embracing a space, as is believed, of about twelve miles in length, and completed their peripatetic labours about half-past four o'clock. This over, the parties retired to various places of festive enjoyment, winding up the proceedings of the day with a plentiful allowance of good cheer.

Other demonstrations of loyalty were general throughout the city. The military fired a feu-de-joie in the Barrack Square at twelve o'clock, and a Royal salute thundered from the Duke of Wellington, steamer. The civic authorities met in the Town-hall, and drank the health of Her Majesty, and other appropriate toasts. The St. Andrew's Society dined in the County Rooms; the Trades, in their own Hall; and the Coronation Banquet, in the Public Rooms, to which the Officers of the 74th Regiment, now in our Barracks, were invited, concluded the public festivities of the day. . . . The Banquet passed off with great eclat.

It was a truly gratifying sight to see individuals of all parties layin
" their disputes all aside," and mingling together in the utmost cordialit
of feeling, in honour of our beloved Queen. . . .

Then came the public amusements of the evening : the roarin,
bonfire, the fireworks, and the illuminations. We may well curb ou
propensity to descriptive expatiation with regard to what passed befor
the eyes of thousands. The bonfire on Castle Street was kindled abou
half-past seven o'clock ; the wonders of pyrotechny blazed, and sputtered
and ranged the empyreum, from ten o'clock till midnight ; a band c
music playing at intervals. . . .

In short, nothing was wanting to give suitable effect to the celebra
tion of the auspicious occasion. The festivities began and ended to th
satisfaction of all parties. The most joyous moments, however, mus
come to a close ; the bonfire died away ; the fireworks were expended
the illuminations ceased to blaze ; and the multitude, pleased with th
proceedings of the day, quietly sought the repose of home—from whic
we sincerely hope that no similar occasion will call them for many
long year.

Aberdeen celebrates the Coronation of Queen Victoria

Dramatic rescue as the "Brilliant" goes down

HURRICANE AND FIRE
SINK THE 'BRILLIANT'

December 12, 1839

THE S.S. Brilliant, one of the regular trading steamers between Leith and Aberdeen, was wrecked at the mouth of Aberdeen Harbour on the morning of Thursday, 12th December, 1839. The details of the disaster are worthy of record.

When the vessel left Leith, about three o'clock the previous afternoon, a stiff breeze was blowing, which increased to a hurricane during the night. Notwithstanding, the vessel reached Aberdeen Bay in the early morning, and the crew and passengers aboard were then calculating upon getting speedily into a haven of safety. A series of disasters followed, however. When slightly to the northward of the Girdleness, between five and six o'clock, a huge wave struck the frail craft, carrying the gallant commander (Captain Wade) overboard, where he quickly found a watery grave. The mate then assumed the command, and it was decided to make for the harbour forthwith. While advancing, the vessel was overtaken by a succession of heavy seas and carried on the south side of the north pier, somewhat within its extremity.

The excitement and anxiety of all on board was now intense—the engineers deserted their engines, the steam escaped rapidly; and what with the darkness of the morning, the noise of the breaking waves, and the general confusion, the passengers were at a loss to know for a time how matters actually stood. By and by the vessel hove up on the under-shoeing of the pier; and heeling towards the north, settled down in a position which providentially admitted of a safe communication being established with the shore. Unfortunately, nobody was on the quay to render assistance, nor was it until an urgent message had been despatched that some of the pilots, with other volunteers, appeared. By this time the vessel had hove close up, and a general rush was made towards the fore quarter-deck, whence the passengers and crew were safely landed.   One poor fellow, a passenger, had his leg broken, and several of the escapes were miraculous.   One woman, who had four children with her, left two in the cabin till she got the others ashore. This having been safely accomplished, she ran back for the other two; but just as they safely reached the quay, the vessel fell off, leaving the woman, cook, and second engineer on board.   Through the cook's presence of mind and energy, a line was made fast round the woman's waist, one end being held by him and the engineer, while the other was thrown on shore.   In this way the devoted mother was pulled ashore, and restored to her children.

The crew being compelled to leave the vessel as quickly as possible, in order to save their lives, without being able to draw the fires from the furnaces, and the blow-off pipes having given way through the ship striking against the stones, the boilers were emptied of water, thus causing them to become so much heated that they set the surrounding parts of the woodwork on fire.   The whole of the after-part was speedily alight, and the fire spread over the vessel.   Every effort made to extinguish the flames proved ineffectual and a fire-engine, which arrived on the scene before nine o'clock, could render no real assistance.   A party of soldiers of the 91st Regiment, then stationed in the city, marched to the spot, and was of much service in preserving order.   By great exertions the cargo was saved from the wreck some of it being considerably damaged, however.   The vessel continued to burn until the fire was extinguished by the flowing of the tide, which entirely broke her up and scattered the wreckage along the coast.

Thus ended the Brilliant, after eighteen years of faithful service; for during the whole of that period she had been immune from accident.   She was built at Greenock on 1821, and was the first regular vessel in the Aberdeen and Leith section.   Her loss—the first of a steamer in Aberdeen district— caused keen disappointment in shipping as well as commercial circles.

TRAGIC VICTIMS OF
FOOTDEE TAVERN INFERNO

December 9, 1840

O N the night of Wednesday, December 9, 1840, a fire broke out in the Victoria Tavern, Footdee, involving the lamentable loss of five lives.

The building in question—an old one, of somewhat peculiar construction—was long one of the most familiar objects in the district. uilt, it is believed, by a Mr. Halliday, shipbuilder, it was afterwards cupied by Mr. John Rae, timber merchant; and here his daughter, the complished authoress of "Home" and other poems, was born. Subse-uently the building was converted into a tavern, and early in 1837 it was nted to and occupied by Mr. James Howie.

On the fatal night the family, consisting of Howie, his wife, two aughters, of the ages of twelve and nine respectively, and a lodger, named homas Marshall, had retired to rest somewhat early. Howie and his wife ept in a small bedroom above the entrance door and lobby, the two girls the "tympany" overhead, and the lodger in one of the garrets. The ght was fine, and nothing untoward about the building was observed till out midnight, when suddenly the cry of "Fire!" was raised by several ip-carpenters who happened to pass on their way to their homes. Dense ouds of smoke were then issuing from the roof and vents of the building, d when an upper window was forced open it was found that the interior as ablaze. When almost simultaneously the ground-floor door was burst en it was seen that the conflagration was practically restricted to the stairs.

Heroic efforts were made to get at the inmates, but the flames and ffocating smoke drove the willing rescuers back. There was no response to the repeated shouts and knocks made from the outside, which seemed confirm the general opinion that the whole five had been render unconscious by the smoke before the devouring fire reached them.

It was providential that two other persons were not also sacrificed the servant maid, who happened to be absent on a visit to friends, and little girl who had spent the day with the Misses Howie. The latter w expected to remain over night, as she had frequently done before; but the evening, as if having a presentiment of danger, she signified a stro desire to be taken home. Mr. Howie fortunately complied with the reque and thus her life was spared.

The suddenness of the conflagration and its calamitous consequenc produced a deep sensation in the minds of the populace, and it was lo before the Footdee fire was forgotten.

Fire fighters at the scene of the tavern inferno

WIDOWS AND ORPHANS
OF VIADUCT DISASTER

September 28, 1846

URING the construction of the viaduct leading from Ferryhill towards the city, a fatal accident occurred on Monday, September 28, 1846. The following particulars of it are furnished in the issue of the " Aberdeen Journal " of the 30th of that month :—

A most painful sensation was excited in this city on Monday last by the sudden occurrence of an appalling accident at these works, now in progress, in the immediate vicinity of the Devanha Brewery. At this part of the viaduct, which is to connect the station in Market Street with the bridge across the Dee, several of the arches had been cast, and from three of them the centerings had been removed for some ten days. On Monday morning about eight o'clock, while eleven workmen were employed on and about these three arches, they suddenly gave way, burying the unfortunate men in their ruins. The promptest measures were immediately taken for their extrication; and in the course of an hour it was discovered that no fewer than seven of the workmen had been instantaneously killed by the falling of the arches, while the remaining four were in life, although more or less severely injured. .   .   .

Among the hundreds who hurried anxiously to the spot on the earliest intimation of the distressing catastrophe, Provost Blaikie was among the first to arrive; and, with much assiduity and humanity, directed the operations of extricating the sufferers from the ruins.
.   .   .   Most of those who lost their lives were, we lament to say, married men with young families. The Directors of the Railway have,

in the most liberal manner, undertaken to defray the funeral expenses of the victims of the catastrophe, and to grant temporary assistance to their widows and families, numbering, alas! about fifty individuals.

In Mr. Robert Anderson's "Aberdeen in Byegone Days" (p. 4), references are made to the accident, and a quotation is given from Mr. John S. Stuart's account of it as appearing in the "Book of the Bazaar of the Railway Benevolent Institution, 1893."

The arches of the viaduct suddenly give way ...

QUEEN LEAVES AMAZED CITIZENS THUNDERSTRUCK

September, 1848

THE bracing summer climate and health-giving properties of Upper Deeside having been brought under the notice of the Royal Family by Sir James Clark, principal Court physician, and others, H.R.H. Prince Albert acquired from the Earl of Aberdeen, in 1848, the reversion of a lease of Balmoral for a term of thirty-eight years, dating from 1836.

When, therefore, it became known in Aberdeen that Her Majesty Queen Victoria and her Consort, accompanied by their children, were to land at Aberdeen on their way to Balmoral, there was an immediate and spontaneous exhibition of loyalty on the part of the citizens. The interest in the event was accentuated by the fact that there had been no King in Aberdeen since the brief call made by Charles II. in 1651, and no Queen since the sojourn made by Mary, the Scottish Queen, in 1562, after the fateful battle of Corrichie, when she stayed in the house of the Earl Marischal, on the south side of the Castlegate. It was natural, therefore, that the hearts of the people should go forth to Queen Victoria, and that an enthusiastic welcome should be accorded to her on the auspicious occasion. The various arrangements were taken up with avidity, all public bodies and families vieing with one another in making suitable preparations. In anticipation of the visit, the late William Cadenhead wrote some verses, entitled " Carle, When the Queen Comes," and beginning—

> Cock up your bonnet, Aberdeen,
> Put on your Sunday's claes and sheen,
> And busk ye trig's a new-made preen,
> Carle, ere the Queen comes!

And ending—

> But why need I distinctions draw?
> We've aye been loyal, brave, and braw:
> Then gie her welcome, ane and a',
> Carles, when the Queen comes!

Her Majesty, Prince Albert, the Prince of Wales, Prince Alfred, and the Princess Royal, accompanied by a suitable retinue, left Osborne on Monday, September 4, 1848, en route for what was to become their " dear " Highland home. Embarking in the morning at Osborne pier on the Royal yacht, Fairy, the party reached Gosport before eleven, and at once proceeded to Buckingham Palace. Having disposed of several items of private as well as State business, including the closing of the session of Parliament, the Royal party bade adieu to Buckingham Palace on Tuesday afternoon, proceeding to Woolwich, where the Royal yacht Victoria and Albert had been specially moored for their reception. This journey and the subsequent embarkation took place amid scenes of much jubilation. The entire command of the Royal yacht was entrusted by Captain Lord Adolphus Fitzclarence to the capable hands of Captain John Cargill, of the s.s. City of London, belonging to the Aberdeen Steam Navigation Company. This signal honour showed the extreme confidence reposed in the Aberdeen Captain, who was perfectly familiar with every yard of the course, and whose seamanship was unexcelled. As convoy were the steamers Black Eagle, Vivid, and Virago.

It was at first intended that the yacht should anchor for the night, but on arriving at the Nore, Captain Cargill determined, if permitted, to take advantage of the fineness of the night (it was very beautiful indeed, the moon shining forth and the stars twinkling in great brilliancy), and her Majesty graciously consenting, the signal was given to proceed.

The Royal yacht left the Nore at nine o'clock at night, passed Harwich at eleven, Lowestoft at two, and Yarmouth shortly before three o'clock on Wednesday morning. The Boston Deeps were crossed between ten and eleven forenoon, and Flamborough Head was reached about four o'clock afternoon. Here the cliffs and prominent headlands were lined with loyal spectators, and numerous vessels, crowded with excursionists, saluted the Royal yacht. The passage along the Yorkshire coast during the day was particularly pleasant. The sea was perfectly smooth, and Her Majesty and Prince Albert seemed to enjoy the prospect, as they spent much of their time on deck. At six o'clock on Thursday morning the bold, rugged shores of Kincardineshire came into view, and at eight the Royal yacht gallantly steamed into the harbour of Aberdeen—the whole voyage being thus accomplished in thirty-nine and one-third hours.

The good citizens, who had been busily elaborating their schemes of decoration, etc., relied upon an intimation which had been made that her Majesty's landing would not take place before Friday morning; and they were taken by considerable surprise when the hurried announcement was circulated on Thursday morning that the Royal yacht, preceded by the Vivid, had been seen rounding the Girdleness shortly before eight o'clock. All were thunderstruck with astonishment, many challenging the accuracy of the intelligence. There was, however, no room for doubt; for the Victoria and Albert, with the Royal Standard flying at the maintop, had sailed direct into the harbour, and proceeded to the entrance of the dock without the slightest delay. Fortunately, the Harbour Engineer happened to be at the dock, letting a vessel through the lock. He speedily recognised the Royal yacht; the lock was instantly cleared, and the Victoria and Albert, passing through, was moored in safety at the substantial wooden jetty which had been specially erected, a little to the west of Church Street, for the disembarkation of the illustrious visitors. The jetty was laid with fine crimson cloth, while in front of it was a magnificent triumphal arch, not quite finished, however, and with its scaffolding still intact.

The sudden and unlooked-for arrival of the Queen completely upset the preconcerted arrangements which had been made for telegraphing the approach of the Royal squadron. No time, however, was lost in setting the bells of the city a-ringing, and getting the Royal Standard hoisted upon the bartizan of the Town House. Many of the shops were closed; and business being temporarily suspended, the populace proceeded en masse to the quay, where, in the absence of police and military to regulate matters, those arriving first appropriated the most commanding positions. In the meantime, an express had been despatched to Haddo House to summon the Earl of Aberdeen, Lord Lieutenant of the county, while immediate notice was sent to the special constables, who, on their arrival, exerted themselves to restore order. After a brief period of anxious suspense, the Queen signified her intention to land the following morning, and that the complimentary address from the magistrates would be received on board that afternoon. These condescending assurances—the announcement of which was received with hearty cheers—had the effect of restoring confidence, and occasioned an immediate renewal of the preparations. A large space was specially reserved in front of the arch for the various public bodies; and a spacious gallery, erected in the form of a vast amphitheatre for the accommodation of the general public, tastefully decorated with shrubs and heather, completed the arrangements at this point. The centre of the Quay was reserved for the exclusive use of the Royal party, a substantial palisade being erected on both sides along its whole extent and up Marischal Street to Union Street. The various streets to be traversed were covered with fine sand, and nothing was left undone to add to the comfort and convenience of the Queen and her suite.

In the course of the morning Her Majesty walked for a couple of hours on deck, attired in a cottage bonnet trimmed with red velvet and lace veil, a light silk gown, and Paisley shawl. The cynosure of all eyes, her extreme plainness of dress greatly astonished the lady spectators, of whom many were gowned and bejewelled in the most expensive fashion.

The Lord Provost (Mr. George Thompson, afterwards of Pitmedden) having offered for the Queen's acceptance the silver keys of the city, and the loyal address of the magistrates having been duly presented, the deputation withdrew, when vociferous cheers were given from thousands of voices. The Queen, appearing pleased with her reception, repeatedly bowed and smiled to the spectators. Noticing the particular interest taken in the Royal children by the large concourse, her Majesty, with much condescension, led them forward to the bulwarks of the yacht, where they were seen by all. This considerate and motherly act evoked shouts of applause.

In the afternoon the Prince Consort paid a visit to King's College, where he received addresses from the Senatus of the University and from the magistrates of Old Aberdeen, at the same time having the honorary degree of LL.D. conferred upon him. He then visited Marischal College, at which also he was pleased to receive an address and the degree of LL.D. He was also admitted by the Town Council an honorary burgess of the city.

Exactly at half-past eight on Friday morning, the Royal party disembarked, and were conducted to their carriages by Lord Aberdeen and Lord Adolphus Fitzclarence. Upon her Majesty stepping on shore, the Royal Standard was hauled down from the mainmast of the Royal yacht and the Union Jack substituted, a royal salute of twenty-one guns was fired from a battery on the Inches, the guard of honour of the 93rd Highlanders presented arms, and the city bells were set a-ringing. It is unnecessary to add that the reception given to the Royal party during their procession through the city— and during the journey all the way to Balmoral as well—was of the most cordial character. The populace turned out in their thousands, and triumphal arches with mottoes signifying loyalty and welcome were prominently displayed at numerous points.

THE JOY OF BALMORAL

The natural attractions of Balmoral seem to have fascinated her Majesty from the outset. She expresses her feelings regarding them in " Leaves from the Journal of a Life in the Highlands " thus :—

Balmoral, Sept. 8, 1848.

We arrived at Balmoral at a quarter to three. It is a pretty little castle in the old Scottish style. There is a picturesque tower and garden

D

in front, with a high wooded hill; at the back there is a wood down to the Dee; and the hills rise all around.   .   .   .

It was so calm and so solitary, it did one good as one gazed around; and the pure mountain air was most refreshing.   All seemed to breathe freedom and peace, and to make one forget the world and its sad turmoils.

The scenery is wild, and yet not desolate; and everything looks much more prosperous and cultivated than at Laggan.   Then the soil is delightfully dry.

The favour for Balmoral thus early expressed by her Majesty increased, and led to the purchase by the Prince Consort, in 1852, of the Balmoral estate for £31,500.   No time was lost in removing the old castle and erecting the present palatial edifice, which is one of the finest of its kind in the North of Scotland.

Queen Victoria is welcomed to Aberdeen

HURRICANE CLAIMS 16 LIVES AT HARBOUR

April 1, 1853

FROM the general stability, superior equipment, and sea-going properties of the vessels, combined with the skilfulness of the crews in command from the captain downwards, the record of the Aberdeen Steam Navigation Company has been particularly free from disasters. The most serious casualty which has occurred in the lengthened history of the Company was that which overtook the s.s. Duke of Sutherland at the mouth of Aberdeen Harbour on the evening of 1st April, 1853, when the vessel was completely wrecked and sixteen lives lost.

The Duke of Sutherland left London, en route for Aberdeen, at half-past seven on the evening of Wednesday, 30th March, having on board 25 passengers, a crew of 30, and a general cargo. The passage up to Thursday night was uneventful and pleasant; but by four o'clock on the morning of Friday the wind had increased in violence, accompanied by heavy rain. The progress of the vessel was not materially retarded, however, and she arrived in Aberdeen Bay on the afternoon of Friday. High-water being still a few hours off, Captain Howling, the master, had to wait for the signal that the bar and harbour entrance channel might be navigated with safety.

It may be here explained that owing to the severity of the gale, the roughness of the sea, and the abnormally powerful flow outwards of water from the Dee, caused by a freshet on the Deeside hills, the bar was in a dangerous condition for shipping. The incoming waves meeting the outward rush at the narrow bar caused a cross current, which greatly increased the danger. When at length the signal was given that vessels might enter, a small vessel faced the ordeal with complete success. This inspired confidence in the minds of those in charge of the Duke of Sutherland. The steamer, being set for the entrance, was making good headway; but, when almost on

D 2

the bar, was struck by a heavy sea on the quarter, and carried somewhat to leeward. A second huge wave struck almost immediately, and carried her further in the same direction. Thereupon the captain, who was personally in command, gave the order to the helmsman to " starboard " ; but although he had the willing assistance of four or five men, the wheel refused to answer. The engines were also ordered to be reversed ; but scarcely had the vessel got stern way when the second sea, breaking completely over her, threw her upon the shelving rocks at the extremity of the breakwater. A hole being stove in her bottom, water rushed in, not only extinguishing the fires, but driving the engineers and firemen, for their own safety, from the engine room. The doomed vessel, thus fixed on the rocks, lay at first broadside on to the breakwater of the pier; but subsequently the stern moved round to the northward, in which position she began to break up, the foremast almost at once going overboard. " At this time there were few spectators of the lamentable catastrophe—probably not more than a dozen individuals, whose feelings may be better imagined than described. Captain Howling, standing on the bridge, was seen giving his orders with coolness to get out the life-boats. While the crew was lowering one of these into the water, there was heard a tremendous crash, and in a moment the forepart of the ship parted from the other near the foremast; but, fortunately, the seamen had all previously withdrawn from it, owing to the violence of the sea and the destructive swinging about of the foremast, spars, and rigging. The stern now settled down into deep water, and a scene was beheld almost too appalling for description. The female passengers were clinging to the rails or spars, and almost every sea was carrying them out of the arms of those who were leading them to the boat. One was observed to leap, in a frantic state, from the poop into the boat, which the seamen had succeeded in getting into the water, and in this attempt was rather severely hurt. Only seven men and a woman got into this boat, in charge of the mate. From the slipping of the rope by which the boat was held to the vessel, she was carried away without getting any more on board ; but after riding gallantly over the heavy surge to the beach, all were landed in safety."

In less than half-an-hour after the vessel struck, the life-boat belonging to the Harbour Commissioners was launched, and, having been efficiently manned, made for the wreck with the utmost despatch.   Unfortunately, this boat, in getting alongside the steamer, received damage in the upper parts, with the result that only fifteen persons—thirteen males and two females— were got off in her and landed on the beach in safety.   Probably four or five others might have been accommodated, but, as it was, scarcely sufficient room remained for the manipulation of the oars.   The passengers still on board had by this time clustered around the starboard paddle-box, the vessel amidships having sunk down solidly on the rocks.   To render relief, the harbour-master had the rockets and life-lines brought into requisition, but unfortunately the rocket would not go off owing to the powder charge having become damp.   The heavy rain, the surf that was sweeping over the pier, and inexperience in the manipulation of the useful invention rendered quite a score of attempts useless. Investigation, however, disclosed the real cause of the failure, which was owing to the escape of the powder; and the defect being remedied, those in charge had the gratification of seeing at the next trial the rocket and line carried right over the ship.   With the line, therefore, the crew on board got off the pier hawser; and after fastening it securely, a party on shore tightened it up.   But it was then discovered that there was no cradle to work with.   In the exciting emergency a temporary cradle was constructed out of one of the the boxes which had floated from the wreck; and this being run out to the steamer, one passenger was safely brought ashore.   It speedily became apparent that the box cradle was unsafe, and in lieu of it slings were con- structed, by which several passengers were suspended from the hawser by the waist, and thus saved.   The captain up to this stage seemed to be managing matters on board with ability; but in his efforts to save a female who had got entangled in the netting of the poop, a quarter-boat swinging from the ropes struck him, and he tumbled down, evidently considerably hurt. This injury doubtless paralysed his future efforts.   Almost immediately afterwards, when communication had been established with the shore, and the rope having become entangled on the lady being conveyed across, the captain, it is believed, with the object of unravelling the rope, swung on to it.   But just as he was warping himself across, a heavy sea struck both him and the wreck ; he was next seen hanging by his hands only, and immediately afterwards he dropped exhausted into the raging surf and was drowned.   So close was the wreck to the pier that the captain's brother, perceiving that he was endeavouring to warp to the shore, shouted as well as signalled to him to return.

The Harbour life-boat being unable to make headway through the breakers again, six seamen, with the most laudable motive, manned a salmon coble, and put off to the wreck.   They had not got far, however, when the boat was suddenly capsized, and five of her brave crew were drowned.   The remaining one fortunately got ashore safely.

By the time that the warp was secured, and those on shore had begun to work the lines, the ship parted abaft the funnel, which was still standing, the main and mizzen masts having both collapsed some time previously.   Dr. Sutherland in his interesting narrative says :—" This was rather a favourable occurrence ; for the midship part, containing the engines, we expected would hold out longer, and from this we might hope to get off all the survivors, although sometimes we had reason to fear that the awful destruction which this part of the vessel was suffering in front would annihilate the whole of it before the last person came off.   Six or seven females and at least fourteen men were taken off in this way ; but of the exact number I am not certain, although each passed me as we released them from the ropes."

The hero of this most lamentable disaster was undoubtedly Duncan Forbes Christie, who occupied the position of chief steward of the vessel. " This brave man succeeded most remarkably in preserving his self-command to the last—making almost superhuman exertions on behalf of his fellow-creatures, and displaying an amount of intrepidity and heroism which it was truly affecting to behold and as universally acknowledged as it was admired." He had not only to superintend many of the arrangements on board ; but, " while labouring himself most manfully, had, we believe, to use all kinds of exhortations, entreaties, and even threats to secure his own safety and that of his fellow-sufferers in their perilous position." He helped in getting the fifteen passengers into the boat, caught the rocket-line, and hauled it in by his own hands. In short he was directly instrumental in saving 19 lives, and was the last to leave the vessel. Mr. Christie's splendid services were publicly recognised, and he was made the recipient of monetary and other gifts. He died 20th June, 1898, at the ripe age of 80.

Among others who rendered special service were Captain Gauld, of the Victory; Mr. John Duthie, shipbuilder; Dr. Sutherland, Dr. Matthew, Mr. Donald, Mr. Clouston, Mr. G. B. Bothwell, Mr. Davidson, father of Mr. George Davidson of Wellwood, and Commander J. N. Strange. The whole city was deeply moved by the sad event, strong expressions being made regarding the defective life-saving appliances. Within a week a private citizen offered a monetary prize for the best invention for the saving of life under similar circumstances.

The sixteen drowned included Captain Edward Howling, the master; Miss Sophia Catherine Bremner, youngest daughter of the late Hon. William Bremner, Dominica, West Indies; Miss Lawrence, Chapel Street; Miss Margaret Paul, stewardess; Mr. Burness, passenger, returning home from the Australian gold diggings, and on whose body a belt with nearly £50 was afterwards found; John Fyfe, chief engineer; George Bruce, carpenter; Peter Ligertwood, second mate, etc., A pathetic interest attached to the death of Miss Bremner, who was returning to Aberdeen to be married to a prominent member of the legal profession. She had her bride's cake and marriage trousseau on board, and her lover was anxiously awaiting her on the pier.

It may be added that the Duke of Sutherland was an iron steamer, built on the Clyde in 1847 at a cost of about £28,000. The cargo was estimated at £8000 value.

FULL STEAM AHEAD FOR GREAT NORTH RAILWAY!

September 19, 1854

THE prospectus of the scheme for the construction of the Great North of Scotland Railway was issued in March, 1845, but it took nearly eight years from that time to overcome the various preliminary difficulties, which included the procuring of Parliamentary powers, the successful fighting of rival schemes, and the arranging for the buying-up of the Aberdeenshire Canal.

Matters having at length been settled for the making of the section of the railway extending from Kittybrewster to Huntly, the ceremony of the cutting of the first turf was arranged to take place at Westhall, Oyne, on the 25th November, 1852. It proved a red-letter day in the history of the Garioch, huge crowds assembling from all the surrounding districts. The members of the Aberdeen Town Council attended, being driven all the way in a spanking four-in-hand. Sir James D. H. Elphinstone, the jovial baronet of Logie-Elphinstone, who was chairman of the Board of Railway Directors, personally extended a hearty welcome to all the visitors, while his accomplished lady performed the turf-cutting in business-like fashion, amidst hearty applause. The interest which the launching of the enterprise evoked, not only in Aberdeen, but throughout the North of Scotland, is aptly foreshadowed in the following opening verse of the late Mr. William Cadenhead's "Railway Carol" :—

> What ho! ye sturdy Burghers,
> Or by the wandering Dee ;
> Or where the Ness down its broad firth
> Rolls onward to the sea ;

Or ye who dwell upon the Don,
  Or Ury's classic shore,
Or ply your crafts with stalwart arms
  In the borough of Kintore ;
Ho ! ye who dwell in Huntly town,
  On Bogie's silver side,
And fling the flashing shuttle
  Or tan the tough ox-hide ;
Ho ! dwellers in fair Elgin,
  Ho ! denizens of Keith,
And ye who won in Forres town,
  Beside the " blasted heath " ;
Rouse up ! rouse up ! ye Burghers all,
  Put on your best array—
This day the first turf's to be cut
  Of the Great Northern way.

The portion of the line from Huntly to Inverurie was first made (the object was to give the public the continued use of the canal from Aberdeen to Inverurie as long as possible), and then was tackled the division from Inverurie to Aberdeen, which absorbed the greater portion of the canal course.

The operations of construction having been energetically pushed forward, Tuesday, 19th September, 1854, was selected as the day for the formal opening of the railway. Arrangements were made for a special train starting from Kittybrewster at eleven o'clock a.m. It was drawn by two engines, and consisted of twenty-five carriages. By it there travelled the directors and leading officials, as well as a number of prominent Aberdeen citizens, amounting in all to about four hundred. The various stations en route were tastefully decorated, and each contributed its quota of neighbouring proprietors and burgh functionaries to the party, whilst at every station the whole population turned out. In several instances the pupils belonging to the schools in the vicinity of the line were ranged in military-like order, to witness the new and fascinating sight. The train was advertised to arrive at Inverurie Station " at 11.50, and, true to a minute, it steamed in, in grand style, amid the shouts of applause and demonstrations of wonder and delight of the large and motley group assembled.'' The inhabitants, young and old, were stationed at every point of the long town from which they could catch a glimpse—if not a full view—of the passing train ; and while it was standing at the station to take up the Earl of Kintore, Provost Davidson, and others, as well as to admit of the engines being watered, the members of the Aberdeen City Band, who were accommodated in one of the carriages, struck up in splendid form '' Scots wha hae ''—the inspiriting strains of which were heard above the snorting thunder of the engines on the resumption of the journey, until distance drowned the intervening sound.

On arriving safely at Huntly, amidst the plaudits of an immense concourse, an adjournment was made to a field near the railway station, where a public banquet was held in a large marquee specially erected for the auspicious occasion. The Duke of Richmond presided, and amongst the leading speakers were the Earl of Kintore, Sir James D. H. Elphinstone, Sir Andrew Leith Hay, and Mr. Lumsden of Auchindoir. The toast of '' Success to the Great North of Scotland Railway and to its early further extension to the North '' was pledged with the utmost enthusiasm, to the unique accompaniment of the whistle of the engines which had been drawn up alongside.

Four days later an unfortunate accident took place. The morning train from Huntly, due at Kittybrewster at a quarter past eight, did not arrive till nine o'clock in conséquence of detention at starting. The usual outgoing train had in the meantime been marshalled at the platform, and the passengers seated in the carriages. There being only one line of rails, the driver of the incoming train had, according to practice, shut off steam and applied the engine-brakes when three-fourths of a mile off, so that he might pull up at the danger-signal fixed half a mile from the terminus. Some hundred yards farther on he had again to stop and transfer the engine from the front to the rear of his train, for the purpose of pushing forward the carriages to the platform. Unfortunately on this occasion the brakes failed to act, and the engine dashed with considerable speed into the front carriage of the standing train, smashing it greatly.   A woman who was seated beside her husband unfortunately fell through the carriage-floor and was killed. Many of the other passengers were injured, and the loss to the railway company in compensation and damage to rolling stock amounted to about £15,000.

All aboard for the first run on the new railway!

SHIP SAILS FROM ABERDEEN IN SEARCH FOR EXPLORERS LOST AT THE SOUTH POLE

July, 1857

ARCTIC exploration had a bold and tireless leader in the person of Sir John Franklin. Entering the navy, he took part in the battle of Copenhagen in 1801, and had charge of the signalling of the Bellerophon during the battle of Trafalgar. Joining the Bedford, he was engaged successively in the blockade of Flushing and on the coast of America. In the attack on New Orleans he was slightly wounded. He commanded the Trent—one of the two vessels fitted out for Arctic discovery in 1818—but the scheme proved futile through the disablement of the sister-ship. Thereafter he was engaged in the exploration of the north coast of America, in which he surmounted many difficulties. Knighthood and the degree of D.C.L. from Oxford were honours which followed. In 1830 he was appointed to H.M.S. Rainbow, receiving subsequently the governorship of Van Dieman's Land. The latter appointment he held till 1843, when he returned to England.

Another Polar expedition being decided upon, Franklin gladly accepted the command. Two vessels—the Erebus and Terror—which had already performed a voyage of discovery towards the South Pole, were fully equipped for the dangerous mission, and sailed on 19th May, 1845. The vessels were seen in Melville Bay on 26th July following, but from that time no direct tidings were received.

At first no great uneasiness was felt, but when year after year passed without the slightest information, the anxiety of the relatives at home extended to the general public. The result was that relief and search expeditions were sent out, commencing in 1848. They continued for several years, but all to no purpose.

The Government ultimately gave the matter up as hopeless, and treated proposals submitted by Lady Franklin in a very cavalier fashion. The noble-hearted lady, whom no rebuff could discourage, determined, in the most self-sacrificing manner, that a supreme effort should be made to trace the explorers, and it is at this stage that Aberdeen comes into the story, as shown by the following advertisement, which appeared in the " Aberdeen Journal " of May 13, 1857 :—

Lady Franklin's Final Search.

The Government having come to the conclusion that the fate of the Crews of Her Majesty's Ships Erebus and Terror requires no farther investigation on their part, Lady Franklin, in accordance with her sense of what is due to the lost Navigators, is now fitting out an Expedition at her own cost.

As a preliminary measure, she sought assistance from the Admiralty, by asking for the loan of the Arctic Ship Resolute, which had been restored in perfect order to our Queen by the American Nation, and also for the gift (as granted in her former Private Expedition) of such Stores from Her Majesty's Dockyards as are available for this special service only.

Compliance with these requests having been declined, Lady Franklin is now devoting her whole fortune to this Final Search ; and a large Screw Yacht, the Fox (built for Sir Richard Sutton, Bart., in 1855), lying at Aberdeen, has been purchased, which the distinguished Arctic officer who has accepted the command of her, Captain M'Clintock, R.N., has pronounced to be perfectly adapted to this employment.   .   .   .

The news columns of the same issue furnish the following further particulars :—

The Fox is built of diagonal planking ; is 320 tons measurement ; 132 feet of extreme length, 25 feet of breadth, and 13 of depth ; draught of water about 11 feet. She is a screw of 30 horse power. Mr. Hall has at present about 100 men employed in thoroughly fortifying and

adapting her in the most approved manner which experience ca
suggest. The screw and rudder are to be fitted with lifting apparatus
suitable for the ice (the engine arrangements being under the charge o
Messrs. Abernethy); and, on the whole, we believe it is Captair
M'Clintock's opinion that, as regards form, size, and general adaptation
as well as sailing qualities, the Fox is the most complete vessel tha
has ever gone on a searching expedition. As far as possible, the whole
equipments will be taken from Aberdeen, as will also most of the
crew, which will number about 30, picked men, who will receive goo
pay. Several volunteers have offered themselves—some even from othe
countries.

The issue of July 8th announces that the Fox had sailed from Aberdeer
on the Wednesday preceding, Lady Franklin having come specially nort
to see her off. An immense crowd turned out to see the way-going, an
best wishes were expressed for a successful voyage.

The " Athenaeum " gave the following additional facts :—

Captain M'Clintock's officers are—Lieut. Hobson, R.N., who di
duty for seven years in the Plover in Behring's Straits; Captain Alle
Young, is sailing-master : he contributed £500 to the equipment of th
Fox. Dr. David Walker acts as Surgeon and Naturalist; and Mr
Peterson, who was with the expeditions of Captain Penny and Dr. Kane
is interpreter. The Fox will put in at Disco to coal, and procure a larg
number of sledge-dogs, a dog-driver, and another Esquimaux interpreter
so as to give additional security that intelligence will be faithfully
rendered. The expedition is provided with the best photographic
apparatus, which will be used by Dr. Walker, who is skilled in the ar
of photography.

In 1859 the expedition discovered a document which had been deposited
about twelve years before, and gave the latest particulars of Franklin'
unfortunate enterprise. The paper was one of the printed forms usually

furnished to discovery ships, for the purpose of being enclosed in bottles and thrown overboard at sea, and it gave the following facts :—

On the 28th May, 1847, when the document was dated, the expedition, after wintering at Beechey Island and ascending Wellington Channel to lat. 77° N., had returned by the west side to Cornwallis Island. At this time all were well. A marginal note, dated 28th April, 1848, told a widely different and pathetic tale. Sir John Franklin had died on the 11th of June, 1847, and the loss by death had been nine officers and fifteen men. The ships had been abandoned three days previous to the above date, having been beset since September, 1846, and the surviving officers and crew, consisting of 105 souls, had proceeded five leagues from the place where the ships were. The Esquimaux reported that all the crews had died, and several bodies and relics which were discovered gave too true a corroboration of the regrettable fact.

At the annual meeting of the Royal Geographical Society on 28th May, 1860, the Founder's gold medal was presented to Lady Franklin and Sir Leopold M'Clintock (he had previously received the honour of knighthood)— to the former as a testimony of " the services rendered to science by her late gallant husband, and also as a token of respect and admiration for the devotedness with which she has pursued those inquiries which have resulted in clearing up the fate of the crews of the Erebus and Terror, and at the same time in making important contributions to our geographical knowledge of the Arctic regions " ; to the latter " in acknowledgment of the very great and valuable services he had performed—services appreciated not only throughout this country, but throughout all Europe and America." Lady Franklin, in acknowledging the honour, claimed for her husband the crowning discovery of the North-West Passage, which cost himself and his companions their lives.

A monument in memory of Franklin was placed in Westminster Abbey, and on it the following lines by Tennyson were inscribed :—

> Not here ! the white North has thy bones ; and thou,
>   Heroic sailor-soul,
> Art passing on thine happier voyage now
>   Toward no earthly pole.

And _Punch_ of 1st June, 1895, had these lines in commemoration of the fiftieth anniversary of the day when the Franklin expedition set sail (given as May 20, 1895) :—

> The North returned thee not to British earth,
>   Whence on that splendid quest thou didst go forth ;
> But when our British hearts, in sordid dearth
> Of pride, forget thy valour and thy worth,
>   Those hearts must be yet colder than the North.

Messrs. Alexander Hall & Company, Limited, shipbuilders, Aberdeen, kindly inform us that the s.s. Fox is now owned by a Danish company trading in Greenland.

The H.M.S. Terror icebound in the Polar Sea

RIOT 'DISGRACE' AT NEW RECTOR'S INSTALLATION

March 16, 1861

FOR many generations university students have recognised that they are allowed a special licence to indulge in fun and merriment at the election, installation, or speech-making of their rectors. Occasionally these revelries have been carried too far—as, unfortunately, happened at Aberdeen on Saturday, 16th March, 1861.

The causes which led to this row were altogether special and exceptional. The first rectorial election after the fusion of the Colleges had taken place (and under a new system of election)—the candidates being the Right Hon. Edward Francis Maitland, Solicitor General for Scotland (who ultimately became a judge of the Court of Session under the title of Lord Barcaple)—the nominee of the King's College party—and Sir Andrew Leith Hay of Leith-hall, who was put forward by the Marischal College section. Sir Andrew polled 240 votes to 202 recorded for his opponent, and thus naturally was entitled to the seat. The nations having voted equally, however, and the Chancellors of both Colleges being dead, it fell to the Vice-Chancellor, Principal Campbell, to decide, and he gave his casting vote for Maitland. Maitland's election was thus regarded as an "intrusion" by the majority of the students; hence the antagonism—and the row.

The formal installation of the Rector was fixed to take place in the Hall of Marischal College. Party feeling ran high, and it was not mollified by Mr. Maitland's allusion to it in his letter declining an invitation which certain of the students had sent him to attend a banquet to his honour to be held on the historic occasion. We abridge the following from the report of the procedure at the installation, which appeared in the " Aberdeen Journal " of March 20, 1861 :—

The agitation which has been kept up with more or less intensity among the students ever since the election, seemed to be brought to

E

a climax, in the case of those who opposed Mr. Maitland, by the ceremony of his induction; for, on entering the hall, greatly more than the
wonted noise and excitement prevailed. . . . Not only did the usual
variety of sounds—some of them comical enough—greet the ear, but
sticks were pitched about freely, without any regard to where they fell.
No kind of missile, so far as could be seen, was allowed to be taken into
the hall; but some of the malcontents had brought hammers or some
kind of tool in their pockets, and they speedily smashed up the seats,
and converted them into fragments quite handy for throwing about.
The forms had been, as usual, nailed to the floor, but this did not prevent the operation referred to.

When the procession, consisting of the Magistrates and Council,
and the Professors, along with members of the University Council,
entered with the Lord Rector, the cheering, hissing, hooting, and
yelling were loud and prolonged, and a shower of sticks, which seemed
to have been reserved for this moment, fell, without respect of persons
or places. Principal Campbell having taken his place at the rostrum,
called on the meeting to engage with him in prayer. A number of the
medical students, however, seemed to evince a determination that the
proceedings should not be allowed to commence, for they hooted,
whistled, etc., for several minutes. At length, at a moment when some
measure of calm was restored, the Principal commenced a Latin prayer
which was interrupted more than once by ejaculatory sounds . . .
which caused laughter. . . . The prayer over, the hooting and
uproar recommenced, during which the oath was administered to
Mr. Maitland.

A protest against the election of Mr. Maitland having been read
by a Divinity student, instruments were taken in the hands of a Notary
Public.

Principal Campbell then shook hands with Mr. Maitland, con
gratulating him on his appointment, and the Rector thereafter ascended

to the desk, upon which he placed the manuscript of his address, during which time the uproar continued unabated. The Rector in vain beckoned for silence, and stood for a time smiling at the hurricane of noise, which prevented him getting further in his address than the first word—" Gentlemen."

At this stage a student mounted on a form and, addressing the Rector, said—" I am requested to inform you by the students of the University of Aberdeen that they hope you will not think of addressing them, as they——." But the noisy portion of the audience did not feel more disposed to hear the student than the Rector, and the Professors began to move off the platform and to remonstrate personally with those taking a leading part in the row. At this time the hooting and whistling had an instrumental accompaniment, sounds like those of drums beating starting out from the other noises; and pease in handfuls and lesser quantities, and occasionally sticks and pieces of wood, were thrown. The Rector kept smiling, and went on—" Gentlemen, I accept—(cheers, hisses, and interruptions)—as frankly as—(hooting)—the protest—(great uproar)—which you (looking to the demonstrators) have just offered." (Uproar.) The protest was here handed to Principal Campbell, who received it. The Rector, still looking blandly, endeavoured to proceed thus—" Gentlemen, I should be entirely——" (hooting and interruption). Here it was observed by those near the Rector that blood trickled down the learned gentleman's face, suggesting that he must have been struck by some of the missiles flying about. The younger, and quieter students attempted, by hissing, to shame down the rioters; and a voice was heard from the platform to " call in the police."

Principal Campbell, advancing to the end of the platform, exclaimed —" I will take other means to put an end to this disgraceful scene. The names of two or three gentlemen who have been taking an active part in these proceedings have been recorded, and——" (cries of " Out with them!" " Expel them!" concluded the sentence). But the row abated not, and someone exclaimed—" Call in the police!" (Great

E 2

shouting, and cries of ''Oh! oh!'') The Principal continued—''I ar
sorry to say some of you have to-day . . . your prospects in life ar
ruined by the proceedings of to-day; some of you not only make use c
expressions of opinion, but use dangerous missiles.''

The tumult continued, a diversion arising through the protestin
students making a rush to leave the hall, which a number of ther
accomplished. The Principal ordered the door to be locked, which wa
done. The police were sent for, and several were brought up to the ha
door, but no force was used by them. Some of the students outside, i
their determination to keep matters lively, commenced throwing stonc
at the hall windows. Ultimately they forced open the door and re
entered. Pandemonium again reigned supreme, and the proceeding
had perforce to be brought to an abrupt termination.

The manuscript of the Rector's address was handed to the press, an
a full report of it subsequently appeared.

Students riot as new rector is inducted

QUEEN'S 'PAIN AND DREAD' AT TRIBUTE TO PRINCE

October 13, 1863

IN no district was the unexpected death of the Prince Consort more deeply felt than in the city and county of Aberdeen. The Prince, who was proprietor of Balmoral and LL.D. of Aberdeen University, had won the esteem of the populace by his unvarying urbanity and dignified bearing, and it was felt that something should be done to perpetuate his memory in the district.

A public meeting was convened in Aberdeen on 23rd January, 1862, when it was unanimously agreed, on the motion of the Earl of Aberdeen, " ' that a memorial be erected in the city to commemorate the public and private virtues of the late Prince, the cost to be defrayed by the voluntary subscriptions of the city and county." The subscriptions having exceeded £2500, it was decided to engage an artist of eminence to carry out the scheme. Baron Marochetti, who was then at the zenith of his fame as a sculptor, was finally engaged, and he personally visited the city and selected the south-east corner of Union Terrace as the most suitable site on which to erect the monument, which it was agreed should take the form of a bronze statue of the deceased, set on a massive granite pedestal.

Everything being satisfactorily completed by the autumn of 1863, and the Queen, who was then in residence at Balmoral, having been communicated with, her Majesty was graciously pleased to signify her willingness to be personally present at the unveiling of the statue on Tuesday, 13th October, 1863. The Court Circular of the following day gives a fairly exhaustive account of the proceedings, thus :—

Balmoral, October 14.—The Queen, accompanied by Prince and Princess Louis and Prince William of Hesse, the Princess Helena and Louisa, and Princes Arthur and Leopold, attended by the ladies and gentlemen-in-waiting, left the Castle yesterday morning at ten o'clock for Aboyne, where a special train was in readiness to convey her Majesty and the Royal Family to Aberdeen to witness the inauguration of the memorial to the Prince Consort. At the Aberdeen Station her Majesty was received by the Lord Provost and city authorities, the Duke of Richmond and a committee of the subscribers to the memorial, Major-General Walker, Colonel Gordon, C.B., etc., and a guard of honour from the 74th Highlanders. Her Majesty and the Royal Family left the station in three of the Royal carriages, attended by an escort of the 3rd Hussars, preceded by the city authorities and the members of her Majesty's and the other Royal households, and proceeded to the Club House to witness the uncovering of the statue of the Prince Consort. At the Club House Her Majesty was received by a guard of honour of the 92nd Highlanders, the subscribers to the memorial, etc. On her Majesty's appearing on a platform erected for the purpose, the statue of the Prince Consort was, after a prayer by Principal Campbell, uncovered, and the troops presented arms. The Queen, after resting a short time, returned in the same order as on arriving, reaching Balmoral at half-past six o'clock, and, though much fatigued by the exertion and trying emotions of the day, has not suffered in health therefrom. . . .

The following additional facts are recorded in Queen Victoria's "More Leaves from the Journal of a Life in the Highlands" :—

" Vicky and Alice were with me, and the long, sad, and terrible procession through the crowded streets of Aberdeen, where all were kindly, but all were silent, was mournful, and as unlike former blessed times as could be conceived. Unfortunately, it continued pouring. The spot where the Statue is placed is rather small, and on one side close to the bridge, but Marochetti chose it himself.

I got out trembling; and when I had arrived, there was no one to direct me and to say, as formerly, what was to be done. Oh ! it was and is too painful, too dreadful !

. . . Then we all stepped on to the uncovered and wet platform directly opposite the Statue, which certainly is low, and rather small for out-of-doors, but fine and like. Principal Campbell's prayer was very long—which was trying in the rain—but part of it (since I have read it) is really very good.

I felt very nervous when the Statue was uncovered, but much regretted that when they presented arms there was no salute with the drums, bugles, or the pipers, for the bands below were forbidden to play. . . .

Took a little luncheon in a room upstairs with our girls, our footmen serving us. After this we left as we came. Affie met us there, and then took leave at the station, William of Hesse joining him. It was quite fair, provokingly so, when we got to Aboyne . . ."

The day was observed as a general holiday, and enormous crowds were in the streets, which were lined by the military and volunteers. At Guild Street Station, where the train arrived, a distinguished company had assembled, and her Majesty, attired in deep mourning, was greeted with respectful loyalty. She was escorted to her carriage, which was drawn by four horses, and formed the twenty-seventh in the cavalcade. The route traversed was by Guild Street, Marischal Street, and Union Street, to Union Terrace. In Union Street and directly opposite the Terrace a grand-stand, capable of seating about five hundred, had been erected. It was filled by a fashionable assemblage of ladies and gentlemen. The " Club House " referred to in the Court Circular was the building at the corner of Union Terrace belonging to the Royal Northern Club, and which was set apart for the use of the Royal Family. The Queen having entered and taken her position, Lord Provost Alexander Anderson was introduced by Sir George Grey, Home Secretary, when he presented an address from the contributors to the memorial. A gracious reply having been handed to the Provost, he was commanded by Sir George Grey to kneel, when Her Majesty conferred upon him the honour of knighthood.

The procession to the statue having taken place, three men of H.M.S. Winchester hoisted the Royal Standard, which had formed the covering, and the statue was unveiled. The Queen gazed earnestly; and shifting her position to the right, looked again on the well-remembered lineaments of the Prince; then, graciously bowing to the spectators around her, retired into the Club.

The Prince is depicted in the uniform of a Field-Marshal, with the robe and insignia of the Order of the Thistle. He is seated in a Gothic chair of state, which is deemed unduly prominent; as also are the jack-boots he is wearing.   The late Principal Sir William Geddes once characterised the statue as "not a man in a chair, but a chair with a man in it."   Adverse criticism of the proportions of the figure, indeed, followed from the day of the unveiling, and time has not modified the feeling of disappointment.

City's memorial to the Prince Consort

HORROR IN WORST STORM FOR FORTY YEARS ...

August 15, 1874

THE early part of August, 1874, proved wet and disagreeable, practically stopping harvest operations, which had just commenced. On the morning of Friday, the 15th, a severe storm of thunder and lightning took place, accompanied with an unusually heavy rainfall. Rivers and brooks were swollen in consequence to an extent which was not equalled for upwards of forty years.

In Aberdeen the storm began about one o'clock in the morning, the rain being preceded by heavy peals of thunder and vivid flashes of lightning. A constable, while extinguishing one of the lamps in St. Nicholas Street, was struck by lightning and rendered unconscious. A house in Albyn Place was struck by the electric fluid, and the gas-pipes ignited, but fortunately the inmates, being awakened by the thunder, were enabled to prevent what might otherwise have had disasterous consequences. The Gilcomston Dam overflowed, causing considerable inconvenience.

The numerous tributaries of the Don rose in furious spate, flooding roads and fields, doing great damage to both. A number of bridges were undermined, and the roads were in places rendered impassable. Large portions of corn and barley were laid flat, and hay was carried off in quantity. The burn of Leochel caused much destruction, additional force being given to it by the collapse of the mill-dam at Corse. At Alford a doctor lost £50 worth of hay, a garden wall was washed away, and a merchant's shop was flooded, causing a loss in sugar alone to the value of £30. The most serious disaster in that quarter, however, was the destruction of the suspension bridge at Montgarrie. When the Don was at its highest, a cart which had been swept off the bank higher up the river struck the bridge in the centre. This formed the nucleus for other debris, which, with the force of the current, pressed so heavily on the bridge that it gave way in the centre, the two halves falling towards the banks on either side. At Kemnay and Kintore the haughs were turned into inland lakes, and cattle and sheep were destroyed.

The Great North of Scotland Railway was flooded at Wardhouse, entailing the stoppage of traffic for some time. A cessation was also caused in the same way between Keith and Elgin.

The mountain torrents running into the Dee were unprecedentedly high. Large masses of boulders were carried down their courses, and deposited at the foot of the hills, and numerous bridges were more or less damaged. At Auchlossan, the portion of the farm which previously formed the loch assumed its old appearance, and where the day before there was a fair field of oats there was instead one vast sheet of water. A little beyond Lumphanan, the burn—which is crossed by the railway—rose to a great height and sapped the foundations of the bridge, a part of which gave way. No trains were run between Banchory and Aboyne on Saturday in consequence. Other portions of the railway were also damaged through being submerged. At the mouth of the Dee, so rapidly and suddenly did the spate come down that several boats were broken from their moorings and washed out to sea.

At Peterhead, Macduff, and other places, much damage was done to fishing boats and their equipments. Various lives were also sacrificed.

Stormy scene

FIRE SERVICE CAN'T COPE
AS EAST CHURCH BURNS DOWN

October 9, 1874

N the evening of Friday, 9th October, 1874, a destructive fire broke out in the East Church, which resulted in the total destruction of the venerable fabric, as well as Drum's Aisle and the fine old steeple with its peal of bells.

Shortly after eight o'clock, as ex-Baillie Daniel and Mr. Alexander Duffus, confectioner, were passing along St. Nicholas Street, the latter remarked, when near the foot of Upperkirkgate, that he felt a strong smell of burning timber, and on looking around they perceived a jet of flame issuing from the roof of the church, followed by a volume of dense smoke. Both gentlemen then ran with all speed to the church, where they found the choir engaged in psalmody practice, utterly oblivious of their danger and of the havoc being wrought overhead. The fire had not yet broken through the ceiling, and no time was lost in giving the alarm to the authorities. In the meantime the gas was turned off. Hose-reels were quickly set, but before the water was got in play nearly the whole roof was in flames, the centre of the fire being about the east sunlight.

Thousands of people congregated to the scene from all quarters, and took their stand in the churchyard and the adjacent streets, which for many hours were in a state of blockade. The feelings of the crowd received a rude shock when it became manifest that the officials of the Fire Brigade were incapable of grappling with the serious outbreak. No proper system in the working of the appliances seemed to be observed, and several of the hose-reels attempted to be wrought were found to be too short or otherwise defective. Detachments of soldiers from the barracks and naval men from H.M.S. Clyde were brought to the scene, the former forming a cordon around the church, while the latter assisted the Fire Brigade.

" By this time portions of the roof of the church had fallen in, and were igniting the seating and galleries, which quickly lighted up the interior with vivid sheets of flame, and sent up into the air huge masses of smoke and fire. The spectators looked with breathless anxiety for means being taken to avert the impending doom of the steeple, but in vain. At twelve minutes past nine o'clock, such was the heated state of the tower that the old clock ceased to beat, and shortly after the flames crept up its eastern face, while from all parts of the steeple issued streams of smoke. Meanwhile the firemen had taken up a position on the roof of the West Church, and continued to play into the tower, which at half-past nine o'clock was a complete prey to the flames, which were issuing out of the louvre windows at the four sides. The steeple withstood the heat for a considerable time, but at a quarter to ten jets of gas-like flame burst out at various places. Presently the lead which covered the oak framework began to run down in a molten stream, and the heat and glare of the red fire, which now streamed out without restraint and leapt up to the weathercock with sudden darts, became so intense that onlookers had to shade their faces for a time. The scene at this time was one of unsurpassing grandeur, and as the thousands of spectators looked on, watching with bated breath for the fall of the burning fabric, every feeling of regret seemed lost in one of admiration. The framework remained for some time in a mass of red fire, and the oak beams, which might have stood for a thousand years to come, seemed reluctant to go. At five minutes to ten the denouement came, and as the huge fiery skeleton fell, it sent up an immense cloud of sparks, some of which were carried by the wind to distant parts of the town.''

The debris fell into the ruins of the East Church, a portion of it carrying away a few stones from the top of the north wall of the church. This, however, was almost the only damage done to the outer fabric.

After the steeple was demolished, the four corner pinnacles, constructed of fine old oak, continued to blaze, but the seat of the fire was in the tower and belfry, where for a long time it raged fiercely, owing to the large quantity of woodwork it contained and the heavy beams used for supporting the bells. Only these bell-supporting beams could be seen, but those in close proximity could occasionally hear the dull fall of what had formed one of the fine peal of nine bells.

The West Church narrowly escaped similar destruction. Between five and seven o'clock in the morning smoke was seen issuing from its roof, and on an entrance being effected through the lead and woodwork, a portion of it was found to be in flames. Some of the joists in the roof had become ignited by the heat in the tower, and this well nigh renewed the conflagration, but fortunately it was discovered in time to preserve the unique edifice from the devastating flames.

The East Church had been rebuilt in 1835, after plans by Mr. Archibald Simpson, an architect to whose artistic taste the city owes many of its most important granite buildings. It was seated for 1700 persons, was in the flat Gothic style of architecture, and cost upwards of £5000. Fortunately, it possessed strength as well as beauty, and the granite walls passed successfully through the crucial ordeal of the consuming fire as narrated.

Fire destroys East Church

DISASTER AS DEE FERRY CAPSIZES — 32 DROWN

April 5, 1876

THE most serious Aberdeen disaster of the latter half of the nineteenth century was that which occurred on Wednesday, 5th April, 1876, when the ferry-boat plying across the comparatively newly formed channel of the Dee, between the city and Torry, was swamped, and thirty-two lives lost.

The day was observed as the half-yearly Sacramental Fast, when general work throughout the city was suspended. The weather proving abnormally bright and spring-like, many thousands of the residenters were induced to get out of doors for the purpose of holding holiday. As usual on such occasions, Torry proved a leading centre of attraction for the working-classes and young people, whose direct as well as most expeditious method of getting there was by crossing the Dee at the ferry-boat. The width of the waterway at the point was only about 160 yards; but, unfortunately, on this occasion a swift and swollen current was running seawards, occasioned through the rapid thawing of snow on the hills in the upper district of Deeside. The flow—estimated at six to eight knots per hour—is understood to have given rise to anxiety on the part of the boatmen in charge, particularly as the crowds of passengers increased as the day advanced.

The ferry belonged to the Aberdeen Town Council, and was let on lease to Mr. Kennedy. No accident in its working had previously occurred, and a large, substantially-built new boat had recently been provided. The new provision of a wire rope, fixed on each bank of the river, and passing along the length of the boat, and doubling over a wheel fixed by supports to its centre (the motive power was secured by the turning of the wheel), was on this occasion put to such a test as it had never before been called upon to

ear.   About mid-afternoon, when the tide was almost half-ebb, the efforts
f the boatmen were taxed to the utmost on their return journey with a
ontingent from the Torry side.   Little order seems to have been observed
o prevent overcrowding; but at best large and excited holiday crowds are
lifficult to regulate.

Shortly after three o'clock the boat left the Aberdeen side with an extra
omplement of 76 passengers, many of whom had forced themselves on board
)efore all those from the other side had got out.   Preceding it was an
rdinary oar-furnished boat crowded with passengers, which, although skil-
ully handled and making the passage rapidly, was carried far down the
iver by the strength of the current.   When the ferry-boat actually started
here was only one boatman on board; but it is understood that several of
the passengers lent assistance in the propelling, if, indeed, they did not
ictually take the starting into their own hands, in their rash anxiety to get
across.   It was noticed by those on shore that progress was very slow at
irst, which is not surprising considering that the gunwale of the boat was
oorne down by sheer weight of the passengers to within an inch or two of
the water.   Nearing the middle of the stream, however, the full power of
the current was encountered, and it rapidly carried the boat so far eastward
that the rope became taut and so much strained as to almost describe the
arc of a circle.   Progress or return then became an impossibility.

Up to this stage the conduct of those on board had been quite orderly,
but their excitement became intense when the boat canted slightly to the
west side, causing water to flow in.   Shouts for assistance were raised by
the terrified passengers, many of whom were now getting more or less
submerged.   The water continuing to rush in, a cry was made to cut the
rope by which the boat was held prisoner, the impression seemingly being
that if this could be accomplished, and way given, the passengers would be
saved.   The rope, therefore, being cut free at the Torry side, such a sudden
momentum was given to the boat that almost in an instant it turned completely over, amid such a scene of terror as has rarely been witnessed.   In
a few seconds everybody on shore stood appalled at the magnitude of the

disaster and at their well-nigh helpless position to render assistance. For tunately several of the passengers, in evident apprehension of approaching danger, had jumped into the river before the actual catastrophe took place All those who had the presence of mind and hardihood to take this step reached the shore in safety. They had the advantage of getting clear of the crowd and of escaping injury by the capsizing of the boat. They had the further benefit, after the accident had taken place, of being drifted by the current back to the upturned boat, and were able to clamber up upon its side. At least seven men were able to save themselves in this way.

Immediate steps were taken to render assistance from both sides of the river. A number of small boats were launched, and were at once put off to the rescue of the men, women, and children, who were now struggling desperately for dear life in the water. "At first the persons immersed were all in a knot—on the heads of each other, it might be said—but the swift, remorseless current soon sundered them far apart; and dotted all over the surface of the water were to be seen the heads and wildly-gesticulating arms of those now battling so fiercely for life. All that human beings could do was done to save them, and the strenuous efforts that were made were a credit to the heroism of our townsfolk, and did honour to our common humanity. Four boats were put off from the Torry side, and one was launched from the Aberdeen side; and with the aid of the second ferry-boat of which we have spoken, some thirty persons in all were rescued, nearly all of whom were exhausted to a greater or less extent. The remainder of those who were saved managed in one way or another to make the shore by their own unaided efforts."

Several of the cases of rescue savoured of the miraculous. A Torry fisherman, on the lookout for the return of his wife, saw her enter the fatal boat, but, being impressed by the conviction that it was overloaded, he shouted to her to wait until the next turn. The warning was unheard or not acted upon, however. As soon as the boat started, the fisherman declared to his father-in-law, who was beside him, that it would never get across, and they instantly proceeded to launch a boat, which they plied into the stream a little lower down.   Providentially they managed to reach mid-stream before the catastrophe took place.   " The unfortunate woman was encumbered with the creel upon her back, and a large number of those who were now in the water seized upon it, bringing her within an ace of being strangled as well as drowned.   Her husband succeeded in catching hold of her just as she was sinking, and pulled her into his boat.   She was quite insensible when rescued, but she speedily came to herself."   This rescue boat is believed to have been the direct means of saving some ten other persons.   A little girl was saved by her own father, who fortunately heard her cries for assistance and saw her floating seawards.   A woman was rescued in an almost similar fashion, being pulled out by a fisherman's wife at the Torry side, towards which she had been carried by the current.   She was greatly exhausted, but with true motherly instinct had clung tenaciously to her infant child, whom she had been carrying in her arms.   A lame man who required the assistance of a crutch in walking, jumped clear of the boat into the river, and at once made for the Torry side.   When approaching the shore, he recalled that he was minus his crutch, and, thinking that its loss would be serious, he turned and swam back, and actually succeeded in securing it.   By this time, however, his clothing had become saturated, and he had much difficulty in pulling himself and his crutch ashore.   He subsequently complained strongly of having lost the half of a flute which he was taking with him in order to spend a pleasant afternoon in the enjoyment of music among the rocks by the sea-side.   A young lad who was on board with his sister made a vigorous effort to save her, but unfortunately he missed her in the confusion, and brought another girl ashore instead.   The hard fate of a boy of about fifteen was greatly deplored by many who witnessed him.   Bravely breasting the current in order to swim to the Torry side, he was within a few strokes of the beach when he suddenly threw up his hands, and sank, apparently as if overcome by cold or cramp.   Just as he was disappearing, a fisherman made a grasp at him from a boat, and thought he had caught the lad's head, but, unfortunately, he only secured his cap.

F

Of the many acts of heroic rescue performed, that of James Brown, mate of the schooner Speed, is worthy of mention. He happened to be on the river in a pleasure boat with his wife and family at the time of the accident. Landing his family, he enlisted the assistance of two fishermen, and by their united efforts they succeeded in rescuing five persons. The salmon fishers in their cobles also managed to save several lives. The crews of other boats likewise rendered excellent service, and, as already stated, were the means of saving many from a watery grave.

It was some time before the bodies of those drowned were recovered. The scenes enacted when identification took place were of the most harrowing description, and would have melted hearts of stone. The community extended the utmost sympathy to the many bereaved relatives, and, along with the public bodies of the city, contributed handsomely to the relief fund which was at once inaugurated. Various schemes were adopted for raising subscriptions, no fewer than three local bards producing poems of considerable merit, entitled " Shadows on the Hearth," " Our City's Sorrow," and " Are any Bodies Found? "

A Board of Trade Inquiry into the disaster was held, and the feeling aroused gave a substantial fillip to the scheme for the construction of the stone-and-lime bridge which now spans the river.

LIST OF VICTIMS

The following is a complete list of those lost :—

1. Archibald Duncan, aged 29, shoemaker, residing in Farquhar's Court, Upperkirkgate ; left a widow and two children.
2. Thomas Gowans, aged 17, stonecutter, residing in Charles Court, Upperkirkgate. He was a brother of No. 12.
3. John Mitchell, aged about 50, gas-works labourer, residing in Torry ; left a widow and large young family.

4. Robert Cay, aged 15, apprentice lithographic printer, residing at 10 Hanover Street.

5. George Dickie, aged 27, stonecutter, residing in Nelson Street; left a widow and three children.

6. William Bain, aged 20, carter, unmarried, residing with his parents at 77 Broad Street.

7. James Leslie, aged 18, combmaker, unmarried, residing at 82 North Broadford.

8. John Alexander, aged 22, apprentice stonecutter, residing with his father at 13 Upperkirkgate.

9. William Shearer, aged 18, apprentice stonecutter, residing in Mrs. Hall's lodgings, 13 Upperkirkgate.

10. James Munro, aged about 40, foundry labourer, residing at 29 Shuttle Lane; left a widow and seven children.

11. Jane Cooper, aged 14, half-timer, residing at 16 Seamount Place.

12. John Gowans, aged 20, dyer, residing in Charles Court, Upperkirk-gate. Brother of No. 2. He contributed largely to the support of his parents.

13. Margaret Selbie, aged 15, millworker, residing with her mother in Gallowgate.

14. John Reid, aged 17, apprentice stonecutter, residing at 38 West North Street.

15. Benjamin Paul, aged 27, plumber, unmarried, residing at 5 Well of Spa.

16. Andrew M'Killiam, aged 17, combmaker, residing at 97 Causeway-end. He was brother of No. 17.

17. George M'Killiam, aged 14, residing in Boys' Hospital, King Street. He was brother of No. 16.

18. John Little, aged 19, plasterer's labourer, residing at Causewayend.

19. James Slora, aged 17, painter, residing with his mother in Ewen's Court, Gallowgate.

F 2

20. William Duncan, aged 10, residing with his mother in Stronach's Court, Exchequer Row.

21. John William Hanson, aged 16, shore labourer, residing with his father in Scott's Court, Regent Quay.

22. George Burnett, aged 18, stonecutter, residing with his father at 16 Virginia Street.

23. James Smith, aged 18, blacksmith, residing with his parents at 30 Summer Lane.

24. George Alexander Young, aged 17, labourer, residing at Williams' Square.

25. Robert Badger, aged 23, seaman and labourer, residing with his parents at the Links Battery.

26. William Robertson, aged 9, residing with his mother at 25 College Street.

27. William Jackson, aged 21, plumber, residing with his father at Deemouth.

28. John Paul, aged 16, newsboy, residing with his parents at 19 Marywell Street.

29. Alexander Smith, aged 17, apprentice cabinetmaker, residing with his father at 53 Summer Street.

30. Henry Paterson Mathieson, aged 21, apprentice cabinetmaker, residing at 95 Chapel Street.

31. James Harvey, aged 19, combmaker, residing with his parents at 9 Hawthorn Place.

32. Jessie M'Condach, aged 13, message girl, residing in Little Belmont Street.

FLOODING AND CHAOS
AS GALES LAST A MONTH

November, 1876

THE year 1876 proved memorable in the annals of Aberdeen for its serious disasters. April saw the loss of thirty-two lives through the capsizing of the Torry Ferryboat, as narrated in the preceding chapter; while in the months of November and December were many successive wind storms of the most destructive character.

The gale began on Monday, the 13th November, and continued intermittently for upwards of a month. The wind, blowing hard from the south-east, speedily had the sea into a tempestuous condition; and, although at this time the Aberdeenshire coast was clear of shipping casualties, two English barques were wrecked further south—one near Bervie, with the loss of seven men; and the other at Johnshaven, with the loss of nine of a crew. The Torry Ferryboat (the same which met with such a lamentable disaster in April previously), now propelled by oars, was carried down the Dee, and was only saved through being run ashore on the south side of the harbour entrance. Extensive flooding took place in the Sugarhouse Lane district, compelling no fewer than twenty-seven families—representing seventy adults and about three times as many children—to temporarily vacate their dwellings and seek shelter where possible. On the initiative of Mr. Daniel Mearns (afterwards Lord Provost), a movement was at once started in the city for the purpose of raising funds to afford relief to the sufferers. The succour extended was of a varied character, and embraced liberal distributions of coal and of bags of sawdust wherewith to dry the sodden house-floors.

After a slight lull, the gale again broke out, and, being accompanied by a heavy rainfall, there was more flooding in the lower parts of the city. A

Cromarty schooner was driven ashore at St. Combs, while a Peterhead schooner was wrecked at Kinnaird Head. All on board the former were drowned, but the six men on the latter were providentially got off in safety. On the 4th December an abnormally high tide was experienced. At the South Breakwater, which was covered by scaffolding for extensions, a succession of immense waves dashed against the hard masonry and swept in a continuous roaring cataract along almost the entire length of the works. The doors of the lifeboat house were burst open by the force of the seas, necessitating the removal of the lifeboat to a place of safety. The upper stones of Abercromby's jetty were torn up and hurled along the channel, while a number of the larger stones were forced out of the North Pier itself.

Flooding again took place at Footdee, and so high was the tide that the waves came dashing against the houses in Fishers' Square, flowing over the roofs in several instances. Terror seizing the inhabitants, they removed their furniture and effects, storing them in what was deemed the only safe place— the church, in the centre of the square. Here the sight which met one's gaze was ludicrous in the extreme—the pews piled up with cradles, tables, chairs, bedding, crockery and other domestic utensils, "and sixty-one homeless men, women, and children in desolate misery, condoling with each other in that the church at least was safe from the destructive powers." The beach bathing station, which had been practically rebuilt three years before, was completely wrecked. The doors of the lifeboat house adjoining it were forced open, and the lifeboat drawn out by the reflux of the surf and knocked to pieces. In the same way the harbour dock-gates were burst open by the force of the waves and rendered unmanageable. The abnormal quantity of water which thus got into the harbour created consternation among those in charge of its vessels, their anxiety being none lessened when the receding tide caused many of the ships to almost topple over and others to hang on their mooring chains in the most fantastic and dangerous positions. There was a subsidence of part of the wall at Provost Blaikie's Quay through the washing away of the foundations. A fissure of nearly two inches in width ran for a considerable distance along the quay in consequence. Half a dozen fishing boats, insecurely moored, were carried down the channel and swamped or dashed to pieces.

On the Aberdeenshire coast the effects of the protracted storm were severely felt. The Norwegian-built schooners Repart and Frederickshall were both lost at Rattray Head, and their entire crews perished. A Montrose steamer was stranded at Arbroath, and a Swedish brig shared a like fate at St. Andrews. A Norwegian vessel foundered in the Firth of Tay with all hands, while a Glasgow steamer went down off Shields with the loss of fourteen lives.

On the 20th December the gale rose afresh, and on the succeeding days increased to such a hurricane as was considered almost unparalleled in these regions. Again there was flooding and much damage to the harbour and other property in Aberdeen. All the railway lines in the north were either blocked by snow or flooded, and the telegraph service was for a time at a standstill. A Norwegian barque was driven ashore at Belhelvie, and the master and three of the crew were lost. A Norwegian brig made an effort to enter Aberdeen Harbour, but, failing, was driven northward and struck the beach to the north of Donmouth. Fortunately the seven men forming the crew were got off safely. Another Norwegian brig was driven ashore near Donmouth, and the crew of nine were drowned. A foreign barque foundered off the Black Dog, all hands being lost. On the Belhelvie sands a brig struck, and the crew of eight were drowned—four of them while attempting to get ashore. The crews of two other vessels which struck near Donmouth were got off in safety, except one man, who fell into the sea and was drowned. Two vessels foundered near St. Combs, and no trace of their crews remained. Two vessels struck the rocks near Cove, and both foundered at once, carrying their crews with them. A similar fate overtook a schooner at Newtonhill, the crew of eight being also lost. There were several wrecks near Stonehaven and Wick, one at Lossiemouth, and seven on the Orkney coast.

In short, it " was one long series of frightful disasters along the whole of the east coast of Scotland. In all, sixty-three vessels were known to have been lost, and the number of lives sacrificed mounted up to the appalling total of 294."

"Facing up to the gale!"

ONE HOUR TO RUIN — EVEN GAS PIPES MELT IN FIRE

April 29, 1882

UR illustration shows the ruins of the extensive New Market ★ building, which was destroyed by fire with startling suddenness on the evening of Saturday, April 29, 1882. This well-known structure, which had been erected after plans by Mr. Archibald Simpson, the eminent Aberdeen architect, measured 315 feet in length by 106 feet in breadth, with the roof rising to 45 feet. The foundation stone was laid, with considerable masonic ceremony, by Lord Provost Blaikie on October 8, 1840, and the formal opening took place on April 29, 1842, when a musical promenade and concert took place, the proceedings winding up with a grand display of fireworks in the evening. It was a striking coincidence that the destruction should take place exactly on the fortieth anniversary of the opening.

The fire originated a few minutes before eight o'clock in the large stall in the upper west-end of the building, tenanted by Mr. Robert Ogg, basket-maker, whose goods were of a highly inflammable character and closely piled from floor to ceiling. They proved a splendid feeder for the blaze, which was materially increased through the unfortunate melting of the gas pipes. The fire quickly ran along each gallery, devouring toys, clothing, hardware, books, and other commodities on sale in the various stalls, and almost simultaneously attacked the open pitch-pine roof, which, being dry as tinder, was speedily consumed. In about twenty minutes from the outbreak, part of the roof next the Green fell in ; and in little over an hour the huge building was a seething cauldron of fire from end to end, only the stone walls remaining intact. The basement floor, or fish market, being fireproof, fortunately escaped the devastation, although considerably damaged by water.

An elderly man, who had been assisting one of the tenants, lost his life in the conflagration, but it is believed that he had been suffocated by the smoke before the fire reached him.   There were several hair-breadth escapes, some of the stall-holders and their assistants, who found egress by the doors cut off, having to jump from windows or to get the assistance of ladders.

The members of the Fire Brigade rendered good service, as also did the military and police.   The fire, however, had too firm a hold before water could be brought to play upon the flames, but the active operations of the firemen saved the destruction of valuable adjoining property, which it seemed at one stage as if nothing could protect.

Around the market-hall floor were thirty-four butchers' stalls, while in its centre the market gardeners and fruit-sellers were accommodated.   In the gallery were some thirty occupants of smaller stores.   Many of these tenants, in the mistaken belief that the building was fireproof, neglected to insure their stocks of goods, and their losses in consequence proved considerable.   The Aberdeen Market Company, to whom the building belonged, had it insured for £23,500, but this sum represented but a small portion of the aggregate loss.   Several of the stall-holders who had good business connections took temporary premises in various parts of the city, and a large wooden building was erected in the Green for the special accommodation of the dispossessed market gardeners and fruit-sellers.   Within a week a number of stalls were boarded off under the north and south galleries of the destroyed building, and were occupied by the butchers, while the butter and egg dealers exposed their wares in the front vestibule.   Inconvenience and loss were thus considerably minimised.

The contracts for reconstruction were settled on May 27, and the work having been proceeded with expeditiously, full re-occupancy was given at the earliest possible moment.   Unfortunately, however, the New Market has never regained its former glory.

DEATH AT THE THEATRE
AS SCENERY CATCHES FIRE

September 30, 1896

N the night of September 30, 1896, a destructive fire broke out with alarming suddenness in the large building in Bridge Place, which had been erected several years previously by Mr. John Henry Cooke, of circus fame. On the abandonment of the circus performances, the building was made suitable for variety theatrical entertainments, and it became known as the Jollity. Thereafter it was leased to Messrs. Livermore Brothers, who gave it the designation of the People's Palace. Seating accommodation was provided for 2000 people, and the structure, which had its front elevation to Bridge Place, was built close up to properties in Bridge Street and Crown Terrace. By many the exits were considered too restricted, but at a test made some time before on behalf of the magistracy—as the licensing authorities—the building was completely emptied of its audience in some four minutes. No danger to an audience from fire, therefore, was apprehended. On the fateful night, about 500 were present, or only about one-fourth of those who might have been accommodated. This was providential; for had there been a crowded house, there can be no doubt the death roll would have been very heavy.

The performance commenced at half-past seven o'clock, and everything passed off successfully till a few minutes after eight, when the stage curtain was lowered to admit of the readjustment of the scenery between the acts. While this operation was in progress, the flimsy scenery caught fire through coming into contact with the gas jets. Instantly tongues of flame shot up to the roof of the building, whence they spread with the utmost rapidity. The cry of " Fire ! " arose from the audience, and excitement ran high. In the meantime the artistes had fled to their dressing-rooms, whence—without waiting to remove the paint and powder from their faces—they quickly made their way to the street. They escaped with difficulty, all their professional paraphernalia being lost. The members of the orchestra got out safely, as also did nearly all the people forming the audience. Unfortunately, however, in the stampede several persons fell, and those behind, in their frenzied determination to get outside, pushed over their prostrate bodies. By this time masses of fire and burning pieces were falling from the roof, severely burning all on whom they fell. But for the brave work of rescue undertaken by willing workers, the number of deaths would have been considerable. As it was, three persons were burned to death, and upwards of thirty injured. Ultimately the death roll reached seven.

Within half an hour of the commencement of the fire the whole internal woodwork was destroyed, and the large building was in ruins within an hour. The suddenness and lamentable results of the disaster gave additional proof of the necessity for having all places of entertainment constructed on the most improved principles for the safety of the public frequenting them.

The People's Palace Inferno

INDEX OF NAMES AND PLACES.

APPENDIX.

In the month of January, 1912, a protracted gale prevailed over the North of Scot
land, causing much damage as well as the regrettable loss of a large number o
hardy seamen.

By the 14th of the month the sea had become very rough, the Dundee steam
trawler Clio being driven ashore on Cairnbulg Point.   At Spey Bay, two day
later, the Buckie fishing boat Sublime was wrecked, and several of the crew perishe
from exposure.

On the 17th inst. the wind had increased to the hurricane force of some 6
miles an hour.   This proved too much for the s.s. Frederick Snowdon, which wa
on passage from Shields to Aberdeen with a cargo of coal.   The vessel was seen i
the bay, but being unable to negotiate the treacherous bar held off, and was ulti
mately lost at Port Erroll, with upwards of a dozen of a crew belonging to Aberdeen

On the 18th inst. the Winstow Hall, a large vessel belonging to Liverpool
foundered at the Bullers o' Buchan, some 54 lives being thereby sacrificed.   Severa
other casualties took place, involving considerable further loss of life.

The *Aberdeen Journal* and *Evening Express*, with commendable despatch anc
enthusiasm, at once inaugurated a " Gale Fund " for the relief of the widows anc
children left unprovided for.   For the laudable object a sum of upwards of £1,30(
was collected in this way within a month.

On the 9th of February, the steam liner Crimond, belonging to Torry, wa
wrecked at Orkney, and through the drowning of the crew no fewer than fifteer
fatherless children were left without their bread-winners.   The *Aberdeen Journa*
and *Evening Express* again magnanimously came to the rescue, and before the end
of March collected no less than £1,172 8s. 11d. as a Relief Fund.

To have collected for these two schemes an aggregate sum of £2,513 7s. 3d.
is at once a certificate of the power of the Press, as well as the good-heartedness o
numerous readers.